PROVERBS EXPLAINED

PROVERBS EXPLAINED

Understanding the Book and Its Message for Today

Samuel Whitaker

Part of the Bible for Modern Life Series

Ascent Press

Published by
Ascent Press

ISBN: 979-8-9997184-9-5

Printed in the United States of America

First Edition 2026

For those seeking clarity in the ancient words of Scripture.

CONTENTS

Disclaimer

This book provides an interpretive overview of the biblical text using historical scholarship and modern analysis tools. It is intended to help readers understand the themes, context, and message of the biblical narrative and is not intended to replace personal study of Scripture

Introduction

Why Proverbs Still Matters

The book of Proverbs is one of the most immediately accessible portions of the Bible. Its short, memorable sayings have passed into everyday language, shaped parenting practices, influenced leadership philosophy, and appeared on wall art in homes and offices across the world. People who have never read the Bible are often familiar with lines drawn from Proverbs — observations about hard work, honesty, the dangers of pride, and the value of good counsel. The book has a way of feeling practical and timeless at the same time.

Yet Proverbs is also one of the most frequently misread books of the Bible. Because its sayings feel so immediately understandable, readers often approach them in isolation — lifting individual verses from their context and treating them as universal guarantees rather than as carefully crafted observations about how life generally works. When a proverb does not seem to hold true in a particular situation, readers are sometimes left confused or disappointed, uncertain what to make of a book that seemed so straightforward.

That confusion is worth taking seriously. It points to something important: Proverbs is a more complex and carefully constructed work than it first appears. The book belongs to a tradition of wisdom literature that flourished across the ancient Near East, and it reflects a sophisticated understanding of how human beings learn, grow, and make decisions. Its sayings were not originally intended as simple rules to follow mechanically. They were designed to cultivate a particular kind of mind — one capable of observing the world carefully, recognizing patterns in human behavior, and making sound judgments in the face of uncertainty.

The book also raises deeper questions. What does it mean to live wisely? Where does genuine wisdom come from, and how is it developed over time? What is the relationship between practical intelligence and moral character? How should a person navigate the reality that careful, honest living does not always produce the outcomes it seems to promise? These are not simple questions, and Proverbs does not offer simple answers. Instead, it invites readers into a sustained reflection on the nature of wisdom itself — its origins, its demands, and its limits.

For modern readers, the world behind Proverbs can feel distant in ways that are easy to underestimate. The cultural assumptions embedded in its sayings, the structure that organizes its very different sections into a unified collection, and the ancient understanding of wisdom as a way of life rather than a collection of useful tips — all of these require some orientation before the book can be read well.

This book aims to provide that orientation. Rather than examining every proverb individually, Proverbs Explained focuses on the broader patterns that shape the collection: the historical and cultural setting that produced it, the recurring themes that run throughout its diverse sections, the structure that holds the book together, and the ways its vision of wisdom continues to speak to enduring questions about how to live.

Proverbs is not a self-help guide dressed in ancient language. It is a serious invitation to think carefully about what it means to live with integrity, discernment, and purpose. Understanding it more fully changes how it is read — and how its wisdom is applied.

That invitation remains open. The goal of this book is to help modern readers accept it.

Chapter 1

The Human Question

*"The fear of the Lord is the beginning of wisdom, and knowledge of
the Holy One is understanding."*
— Proverbs 9:10 (NIV)

The Universal Search for Wisdom

Across cultures and throughout history, human beings have
recognized that knowing facts is not the same as knowing how to
live. A person can accumulate a great deal of information about
the world and still make decisions that harm themselves and
others. A person can be highly educated and still lack the
judgment to navigate difficult relationships, the discipline to resist
self-destructive patterns, or the discernment to distinguish
between what seems good and what actually is good. The gap
between knowledge and wisdom has always existed, and people in
every culture have tried to close it.

Ancient societies developed many ways of passing
accumulated wisdom from one generation to the next.
Experienced elders offered counsel to younger members of their
communities. Parents instructed children in the habits and values
that shaped a good life. Teachers gathered observations about
human behavior into memorable forms that could be learned,
repeated, and applied. These traditions recognized something
important: wisdom is not simply inherited. It must be taught,
cultivated, and practiced. And the teaching of wisdom — the craft
of shaping minds capable of good judgment — has always been
one of the most important tasks any community undertakes.

The book of Proverbs belongs to this universal human
endeavor. It is one of the oldest and most developed examples of

wisdom instruction in the ancient world, preserving sayings, teachings, and extended reflections that were designed to form the kind of person who could live well, not just successfully by outward measures, but with integrity, discernment, and a clear sense of what genuinely matters. Understanding Proverbs well begins with recognizing what it was trying to do and for whom it was originally written.

This deeply practical orientation has helped Proverbs remain accessible across centuries. People continue to return to its sayings because they recognize something immediately useful within them. The observations about pride and humility, hard work and laziness, honest speech and deception — these touch areas of life that remain as relevant today as they were three thousand years ago. Yet as accessible as Proverbs feels at the surface level, there is considerably more depth beneath those familiar lines than most readers initially realize.

The Search for the Good Life

One of the oldest and most persistent questions human beings have asked is deceptively simple: what does it mean to live well? This question appears across every culture and every historical period, addressed by philosophers, religious traditions, poets, and parents in vastly different ways. Some answers have focused on pleasure, arguing that a good life is one that maximizes happiness and minimizes suffering. Others have emphasized duty, suggesting that living well means fulfilling obligations to family, community, and the divine. Still others have located the good life in virtue — in the development of character traits that produce both personal flourishing and positive relationships with others.

These different answers are not simply competing philosophical positions. They reflect genuinely different understandings of what human beings are, what we need, and what we are capable of. The question of how to live well is not merely abstract. It shapes the daily decisions people make about how to spend their time, who to trust, what to pursue, and what to refuse. Every person who gets out of bed in the morning and moves through a day is, in some sense, enacting an answer to this question — whether or not they have ever consciously thought about it.

The book of Proverbs approaches this question with unusual directness. Rather than constructing philosophical arguments, it offers accumulated observations drawn from careful attention to how life actually unfolds for human beings over time. The sages who produced this material were paying attention to patterns in human behavior, to the consequences of different kinds of choices, to the traits of character that seemed consistently to lead toward flourishing and those that seemed consistently to lead toward ruin. What they observed, they collected. What they collected, they shaped into memorable forms. And what they shaped, they passed on to the next generation with a clear intent: to form people capable of living wisely in a complex world.

This approach gives Proverbs a quality that distinguishes it from more systematic forms of instruction. It does not begin with abstract principles and deduce applications. It begins with observable reality — with what actually happens when people act with honesty or deception, with diligence or laziness, with humility or pride — and works from there toward broader understanding. The result is a body of teaching that feels grounded rather than theoretical, earned rather than assumed.

Speaking Through Observation

Another striking feature of Proverbs is the way it communicates. Rather than offering lengthy explanations or detailed arguments, it relies heavily on brief, carefully crafted sayings that compress a great deal of insight into very few words. A proverb is not simply a short sentence. It is a sentence designed to be remembered, repeated, tested against experience, and deepened through use over time. The best proverbs do not exhaust their meaning on first encounter. They reward return. Each time a reader encounters a proverb in a new situation, the saying can reveal a dimension that was not visible before.

This form of communication requires something from the reader. A proverb is not meant to be passively received. It is meant to be turned over in the mind, tried against real experience, and engaged with actively. When a saying from Proverbs seems self-evident on first reading, that feeling of recognition is not the end of the encounter — it is the beginning. The reader who asks what else the saying might mean, what situations it applies to, and what its limits might be is engaging with the text in the way it was designed to be used.

The form also requires a kind of interpretive judgment that is itself part of the wisdom the book is trying to develop. Two proverbs that seem to contradict each other — a feature of Proverbs that has puzzled many readers — are not evidence of careless editing or inconsistent thinking. They are a deliberate invitation to discernment. Real wisdom does not consist of memorizing correct answers and applying them mechanically to every situation. It consists of knowing which insight applies in which circumstances, and that kind of contextual judgment is precisely what Proverbs is trying to cultivate. The apparent contradictions are teaching tools.

For modern readers, this can feel initially frustrating. We often prefer clear, consistent guidance — rules that can be followed without ambiguity. Proverbs resists that preference. It offers patterns and principles, but it leaves the work of application to the reader. This is not a deficiency. It is the point. A book that made every decision for its reader would produce dependence, not wisdom. Proverbs is trying to produce wisdom.

Addressing God in Practical Life

One of the most important features of the wisdom tradition that Proverbs represents is the way it understands the relationship between practical life and faith. In the modern world, it is common to think of religious belief as one sphere of life and practical decision-making as another. We often separate questions of faith from questions about career, money, relationships, and daily habits, treating them as belonging to different categories.

Proverbs does not make this separation. For the sages who produced this material, the fear of the Lord — a phrase that appears repeatedly throughout the book and that the text explicitly identifies as the beginning of wisdom — was not a preliminary religious statement made before getting to the practical material. It was the foundation of the entire enterprise. Wisdom, in the understanding that shapes this book, is not a purely human achievement arrived at through careful observation alone. It is a gift that becomes available to those who are rightly oriented toward God.

This does not mean that Proverbs ignores practical observation. It is one of the most observationally grounded books in Scripture. But the observations are made within a framework that understands the world as created and ordered by a God who is wise and whose wisdom is, at least in part, accessible to human beings who seek it with appropriate humility. The fear of the Lord is not terror. It is a posture — an acknowledgment that human beings are not the measure of all things, that there is a larger order of reality than any individual can fully grasp, and that genuine wisdom begins with that recognition rather than with self-reliance.

This posture changes the entire character of the search for wisdom. A person who approaches life with the assumption that they can figure everything out through their own intelligence alone will tend toward the kind of pride and overconfidence that Proverbs consistently identifies as dangerous. A person who approaches life with genuine humility — who recognizes the limits of their own understanding and remains teachable — is already positioned to learn. The fear of the Lord is not the opposite of practical wisdom. It is the condition that makes genuine practical wisdom possible.

The Shape of the Wise Life

What emerges from the opening pages of Proverbs is not simply a set of instructions to follow but a portrait of a particular kind of person — someone whose habits of mind, patterns of behavior, and fundamental orientation toward the world and toward God have been shaped in a specific direction. The book calls this person wise, and it spends considerable energy making clear what that designation means and does not mean.

Wisdom in Proverbs is not primarily an intellectual quality. The wise person is not distinguished by superior intelligence or greater access to information. What distinguishes them is character — a formed way of being that expresses itself consistently across the different domains of life. The wise person is honest not because honesty always serves their immediate interests but because their character has been shaped in a way that makes deception feel like a violation of who they are. They are generous not because they have calculated that generosity will pay off but because their orientation toward others has been formed in a way that makes the need of another person genuinely compelling. They are diligent not because they are driven by anxiety about outcomes but because the discipline of consistent effort has become part of how they understand their responsibilities and take them seriously.

This portrait of the wise life is cumulative. No single proverb captures it fully. It is built up across the entire book through the accumulation of specific observations about specific situations — each one adding a detail, shading in a dimension, showing what wisdom looks like from one more angle. By the time the reader has moved through the full collection and arrived at the closing poem, the portrait is complete. Not as a static image but as a living person — someone whose diligence, honesty, generosity, and care for others are not separate virtues but expressions of a single integrated character shaped by the fear of the Lord.

For modern readers, this cumulative portrait is one of the most valuable things the book offers. We live in a culture that tends to treat the different domains of life as separate — professional life, personal relationships, financial behavior, spiritual practice — as though they can be managed independently of one another and evaluated by different standards. Proverbs insists on their unity. The same character that makes a person trustworthy in their business dealings is the character that makes them a reliable friend. The same habits of honesty that shape their speech in public shape how they speak about others in private. The same orientation toward the vulnerable that appears in their generosity with resources appears in how they exercise whatever authority they hold. Character is not compartmentalized. It expresses itself everywhere, and Proverbs is designed to develop it from the inside out.

This is also why the book begins where it does — with the fear of the Lord as the foundation. The portrait of the wise life that the book builds across its pages is not achievable by willpower alone. It requires a fundamental reorientation toward God that changes how a person understands themselves, their responsibilities, and the world they inhabit. Without that reorientation, the individual virtues the book commends remain disconnected and fragile — useful in circumstances where they happen to be convenient, but unlikely to hold in the situations where they cost something. With it, they become expressions of a coherent character grounded in something more durable than self-interest. That is the foundation Proverbs is laying from its very first lines, and everything the book goes on to say is built upon it.

Individual Experience and Community Formation

Although many of Proverbs' sayings sound as though they are addressed to individuals, the book was not written solely for private reflection. The wisdom tradition that produced Proverbs was deeply communal in character. These teachings were passed from parents to children, from teachers to students, from one generation to the next within communities that understood the formation of character as a shared responsibility.

A young person who internalized the teachings of Proverbs was not simply gaining personal advantage. They were being shaped to contribute to the health and integrity of their community — to be someone who could be trusted, who dealt honestly, who used their abilities in service of others as well as themselves, and who recognized that individual flourishing is bound up with the flourishing of the community as a whole. Proverbs does not imagine the wise person as a solitary achiever. It imagines them as someone deeply embedded in relationships, exercising wisdom in the texture of daily life together with others.

This communal dimension is easy to miss when the sayings are read in isolation. But it comes through clearly when the book is read as a whole. The concern for honest speech, for fair dealing in commerce, for kindness toward the poor, for faithfulness in friendship — all of these point toward a vision of wisdom that is fundamentally relational. The wise person is not merely the person who makes good decisions for themselves. They are the person whose character makes the lives of those around them better.

A Language for the Life Well Lived

Perhaps the most enduring contribution of Proverbs is the vision it offers of what human life is capable of becoming. In a world that often reduces success to wealth, status, or power, Proverbs consistently redirects attention toward something deeper: the quality of character from which all genuinely good outcomes flow. A good name, in the understanding of this book, is worth more than great riches. Integrity maintained under pressure is a greater achievement than any external success. The person who is honest, teachable, diligent, and genuinely concerned for others is, in the deepest sense, the person who has learned to live well.

This vision is not naive. Proverbs is not a book that promises easy outcomes to those who follow its teaching. It is a book that takes seriously the complexity and unpredictability of life while still insisting that character matters, that choices have consequences, and that the habits of mind and behavior we develop shape the kinds of people we become over time. It invites readers to take that shaping seriously — to invest in the slow, deliberate work of becoming wiser, more honest, more discerning, and more genuinely useful to the world around them.

That invitation is as relevant now as it was when these sayings were first collected and passed on. The circumstances of life have changed enormously. The basic challenges of human character have not.

In the chapters that follow, we will examine the historical setting in which Proverbs emerged, the structure that organizes its diverse sections, and the themes that connect its wide-ranging observations about human life. Through this exploration, readers will gain a clearer understanding of how Proverbs functions not only as a collection of useful sayings but as a carefully shaped invitation to the lifelong pursuit of wisdom.

Chapter 2

Orientation

"For the Lord gives wisdom; from his mouth come knowledge and understanding. He holds success in store for the upright, he is a shield to those whose walk is blameless."
— Proverbs 2:6–7

When readers first encounter the book of Proverbs, it often feels noticeably different from many of the other books that appear in the Bible. Some biblical books unfold through narrative, tracing sequences of events that gradually reveal a story about people, places, and historical developments. Genesis describes the origins of the world and the earliest generations of humanity, presenting stories about creation, family conflict, migration, and covenant. Exodus continues that narrative by describing the liberation of Israel from slavery in Egypt and the formation of a new community shaped by laws and shared identity.

The historical books that follow trace that story forward — recording the establishment of the monarchy, the rise and fall of individual kings, the fracturing of the nation, and the slow drift toward exile. Each event connects to what came before and shapes what comes after. The prophetic books work within that same historical framework, addressing specific moments of national crisis with urgent calls to faithfulness and warnings about the consequences of turning away from God. In both cases, the reader's sense of orientation comes from following a story.

Against this background, the book of Proverbs stands apart. Instead of presenting a continuous storyline or a sequence of historical events, Proverbs gathers together a varied collection of sayings, extended poems, and wisdom instructions written at different moments and for different purposes. The book does not follow a narrative arc from beginning to end. It is not the story of a particular person or nation. It is a sustained invitation to think carefully about how life works — and how to live it well.

Because of this structure, readers experience Proverbs differently from narrative books. Rather than following a story, the reader encounters a series of observations, instructions, and reflections that move across a wide range of practical concerns. One passage may address the management of household finances, while the next turns to the dangers of dishonest speech, and the next reflects on the character of a wise leader. The scope is wide because the vision of wisdom that shapes the book is wide — it touches every dimension of human life.

For this reason, many people approach Proverbs as a resource to dip into rather than as a book to read in sequence. Particular sayings become associated with particular situations, and readers return to them as needed. This pattern of reading is understandable — it reflects the genuine usefulness of individual proverbs to speak into specific circumstances. But it can also create the impression that the book is simply a loose collection of useful observations, assembled without a larger structure or purpose.

In reality, Proverbs is far more carefully organized than it might first appear. The book contains several distinct sections, each with its own character, audience, and purpose. Those sections were eventually brought together into the unified collection now preserved in Scripture. The editors who assembled the book were not working randomly. They shaped a text that moves with purpose — from extended instruction about the nature and value of wisdom, through vast collections of practical observations, to carefully crafted poems that bring the whole vision to completion. Understanding that structure helps readers engage with Proverbs as the coherent and serious work it actually is.

A Collection That Developed Over Time

Another feature that distinguishes Proverbs from many other biblical books is the way the collection developed gradually across a long period of history. Unlike writings produced by a single author during a brief historical window, Proverbs emerged through the contributions of many individuals who lived in different generations and wrote for different purposes.

The book itself preserves evidence of this development. Several distinct sections within Proverbs are introduced with their own headings, identifying different sources and periods of composition. The opening chapters of the book — chapters one through nine — consist of extended poetic instructions addressed from a parent to a child, with wisdom personified as a woman speaking publicly in the streets and at the city gates. These chapters have the character of a carefully composed introduction, written to frame everything that follows.

The next major section — chapters ten through twenty-two — is introduced as the proverbs of Solomon, and it contains the dense collections of short, two-line observations that most people associate with the book. A later section, beginning in chapter twenty-five, is introduced as more proverbs of Solomon, copied by the men of Hezekiah — a reference that places its compilation during the reign of King Hezekiah in the eighth century BCE. Still other sections, at the end of the book, are attributed to figures named Agur and Lemuel, and the book concludes with an extended poem about a woman of noble character.

This variety of sources and periods is not a sign of disorder. It reflects the nature of the wisdom tradition itself — one that accumulated observations across generations, preserving insights from many different voices within a shared framework of values and belief. The sages who eventually brought these collections together into a single book made deliberate choices about how to arrange the material, and those choices shaped the meaning of the whole.

The Five Major Sections of Proverbs

One of the most useful ways to orient oneself in the book of Proverbs is to recognize its major structural divisions and understand what each contributes to the whole.

The structure appears as follows:

- Chapters 1–9 — The Extended Wisdom Poems
- Chapters 10–22:16 — The Proverbs of Solomon, First Collection
- Chapters 22:17–24:34 — The Words of the Wise
- Chapters 25–29 — The Proverbs of Solomon, Second Collection
- Chapters 30–31 — The Words of Agur and Lemuel, and the Capable Woman Poem

Each section has its own distinct character. The opening chapters are the most literary and extended, developing a sustained argument for the value of wisdom through poetry, personification, and direct address. The two large middle collections are the densest and most varied, containing hundreds of short observations on virtually every aspect of practical life. The closing chapters bring the book to a conclusion that is both theologically serious and remarkably human in its final image — a woman whose entire life embodies the wisdom the book has been commending throughout.

This five-part movement gives the book a shape that rewards reading from beginning to end, even as it also sustains the kind of selective engagement that most readers bring to it. The opening chapters provide the framework within which all the individual sayings are meant to be understood. Without that framework, the sayings can appear as disconnected observations. Within it, they become expressions of a coherent vision of what human life is capable of becoming.

The Role of Solomon

Perhaps the most prominent figure associated with the book of Proverbs is Solomon, the son of David who ruled Israel during the tenth century BCE. The book opens by identifying itself as the proverbs of Solomon, and his name appears at the introduction of two of the book's major sections. In the broader biblical tradition, Solomon became the symbol of wisdom — the king who asked God for understanding rather than wealth or power, and whose reputation for wisdom drew visitors from distant nations.

The association of Solomon with the wisdom tradition runs deep in Scripture, and it is not arbitrary. During Solomon's reign, Israel experienced a period of relative prosperity and international engagement that would have encouraged the development of a sophisticated court culture — including the kind of scribal and literary activity that produced and collected wisdom literature. The international connections of Solomon's court also brought Israel into contact with wisdom traditions from Egypt, Mesopotamia, and surrounding regions, some of which are reflected in the content and form of the material preserved in Proverbs.

At the same time, scholars have long recognized that Solomon could not have written the book of Proverbs in its entirety. The explicit references to multiple sources and different periods of compilation make clear that the collection grew over time. Solomon's name and legacy functioned as the symbolic center of the tradition rather than as a claim of single authorship. He became, in the memory of Israel, the one who embodied what wisdom could look like in a life — and that symbolic weight shaped how the tradition understood itself and presented its material.

A Book of Instruction

From their earliest context, the sayings and poems of Proverbs functioned as tools of education and formation within Israelite society. The opening chapters make this educational purpose explicit, framing the entire book as instruction passed from a parent to a child — a father's voice calling a son to receive wisdom before life's choices demand it. This framing was not merely literary. It reflected the actual social setting in which wisdom was transmitted: within households, through extended relationships between teachers and students, and eventually through the kind of formal scribal education associated with the royal court.

The educational intent of Proverbs is not limited to the transfer of information. Its goal is formation — the shaping of a person's character, habits of mind, and patterns of response. A student who internalized the teaching of Proverbs was not simply acquiring a set of rules to apply mechanically. They were being formed into a particular kind of person: someone who had developed the habit of careful observation, the discipline to resist short-term temptation for longer-term good, the skill of honest and constructive speech, and the humility to recognize the limits of their own understanding.

This formative intent remains one of the most distinctive features of the book. Proverbs is not merely trying to inform its readers. It is trying to make them wiser.

Poetry as a Way of Forming Character

Another reason Proverbs stands apart from many other biblical books is its sustained use of poetry and literary artistry in the service of practical instruction. Unlike straightforward commands or explanations, the poetic forms that Proverbs employs are designed to do more than communicate information — they are designed to make that information stick, to make it feel true before it is fully understood, and to return to the reader's mind unbidden when a relevant situation arises.

The short two-line saying that characterizes much of Proverbs works through compression and contrast. An observation is made, then sharpened against its opposite. A pattern is identified, then turned to reveal its implications. These techniques do not merely describe reality — they train the mind to perceive it differently. A reader who has spent time with Proverbs begins to develop habits of observation and judgment that go beyond the specific sayings they have memorized.

The extended poems in chapters one through nine work differently but toward the same end. The personification of Wisdom as a woman calling out in the streets, inviting the simple to turn aside from foolishness and learn, is not merely a literary device. It creates an imaginative encounter with wisdom as something alive and active — something that pursues the reader rather than waiting passively to be found. The vividness of that image leaves a different kind of impression than a simple instruction would. It makes wisdom feel like a person one could either respond to or ignore — and the stakes of that choice feel correspondingly personal and real.

The Emotional Depth of Proverbs

Although Proverbs is often understood primarily as a practical book, it also contains a depth of emotional awareness that is easy to overlook. The book recognizes the complexity of human inner life — the way hope, anxiety, pride, shame, and longing all shape the decisions people make and the kind of people they become over time.

Several sayings in Proverbs observe directly that what goes on inside a person is more significant than any external circumstances. Hope deferred, the book notes, makes the heart sick. A crushed spirit dries up the bones. The inner life is not a private matter that has no bearing on practical outcomes. It is the soil from which practical outcomes grow. Proverbs takes seriously the connection between the condition of a person's heart and the direction of their life — and it repeatedly directs attention inward, to the habits of thought and feeling that shape character over time.

This emotional awareness makes Proverbs a more personally demanding book than it might first appear. It is not content with behavioral compliance. It reaches toward the formation of a person whose inner life is genuinely aligned with what wisdom commends — whose honesty is not merely strategic, whose generosity is not merely performative, and whose fear of the Lord is not merely conventional. The standard the book holds out is high, and it is ultimately a standard of character rather than conduct.

The Movement Within Proverbs

Although the book of Proverbs does not unfold as a narrative, there is a discernible movement across its major sections that rewards attention. The opening chapters establish the framework within which everything else is meant to be understood — wisdom is personified, its value is argued for at length, and the reader is repeatedly invited to choose it above everything else the world offers.

The great central collections that follow then demonstrate what wisdom looks like in practice — in small, concrete, observable situations that accumulate into a portrait of the wise life. And the closing chapters bring the book to a conclusion that is both theologically grounding and humanly specific: a figure named Agur acknowledging the limits of his own understanding, a king's mother instructing her son in the character of a good ruler, and finally a sustained poem describing a woman whose life has become the embodiment of everything the book has been commending.

That closing poem is not an afterthought. It is a completion. The wisdom that was personified as a woman calling out at the beginning of the book finds its human expression at the end — not in abstract virtue, but in a specific life shaped by diligence, generosity, wisdom in speech, and genuine care for the people around her. The book ends where all genuine wisdom ends: not in ideas, but in character expressed through action.

Preparing to Understand Proverbs

Recognizing these features of the book of Proverbs provides a foundation for deeper engagement with the material in the chapters that follow. Understanding that the collection developed gradually, that it contains several distinct sections with different characters and purposes, that it was designed for education and formation rather than mere information transfer, and that it functions through literary artistry as well as direct instruction — these realities together help readers approach the text with greater awareness and realistic expectations.

Rather than expecting Proverbs to behave like a systematic rulebook or a guaranteed formula for success, readers can appreciate it as a carefully crafted body of wisdom shaped by real experience across many generations. The sayings do not offer mechanical solutions. They invite readers into a process of formation that unfolds over time — sometimes over a lifetime of returning to the same passages and finding that they have something new to say.

The book becomes, in this light, not merely a collection of useful observations but a carefully designed school for wisdom — one that is patient enough to teach through indirection, artistry, and accumulated insight rather than through commands alone.

In the next chapter, we will step into the world that produced these sayings and poems. The cultural and social realities of ancient Israel and the wider ancient Near East shaped the experiences and observations that gave rise to Proverbs, and understanding that world reveals why this material took the particular form it did — and why that form has proven so enduring.

Chapter 3

The World Behind the Book

"By wisdom the Lord laid the earth's foundations, by
understanding he set the heavens in place; by his knowledge the
watery depths were divided, and the clouds let drop the dew."
— *Proverbs 3:19–20*

Life in Ancient Israel

Understanding the book of Proverbs becomes considerably easier when readers step back and consider the historical world in which its sayings and poems first emerged. Although the observations about human behavior preserved in Proverbs remain strikingly recognizable to modern readers, the cultural and social environment that shaped this material was very different from the world most people experience today. Ancient Israel existed within a landscape defined by agriculture, kinship networks, political vulnerability, and a deeply integrated understanding of the relationship between everyday life and faithfulness to God. Communities were smaller, communication moved slowly, and the rhythms of existence were closely tied to seasons of planting, harvest, and the social obligations that held families and villages together.

In such a world, the consequences of good and poor judgment were often immediate and concrete. A person who managed their household resources wisely could sustain their family through difficult seasons. A person who borrowed recklessly, made alliances carelessly, or allowed personal discipline to erode could face consequences that affected not only themselves but everyone who depended on them. In a society without the complex safety nets of the modern world, practical wisdom was not a luxury or an intellectual interest. It was a survival skill — and it was taken seriously as such.

The sages who produced the material preserved in Proverbs were paying attention to these realities. They observed what happened to people over time — which habits of character led consistently toward flourishing, which patterns of behavior led consistently toward destruction, and which qualities distinguished the kind of person a community could trust and rely upon from the kind it could not. What they observed, they shaped into memorable form and passed on. Understanding the world they were observing helps readers understand why the book says what it says.

Daily Life and the Household

To understand the content and emphasis of Proverbs, it helps to consider the rhythms of daily life more closely — and in particular, the central importance of the household in ancient Israelite society. Unlike modern societies organized primarily around individual achievement and institutional frameworks, ancient Israelite life was structured primarily around the household — the extended family unit that included not only parents and children but also servants, dependent relatives, and the economic activity that sustained them all.

The household was the fundamental unit of production, consumption, education, and social stability. Its success depended on the coordinated effort and wise management of everyone within it. Land needed to be cultivated, animals tended, resources preserved and allocated carefully across seasons, and the next generation raised with the skills and values that would allow them to sustain what had been built. In this context, the kind of wisdom Proverbs commends was not abstract but thoroughly practical — it was wisdom expressed in the daily management of relationships, resources, and responsibilities.

This household context explains the prominence of certain themes in Proverbs that might otherwise seem mundane. The repeated attention to diligence versus laziness, to honest weights and measures in commercial dealings, to the care of the poor within one's community, and to the management of speech in close relationships — all of these reflect the specific concerns of people responsible for the complex web of relationships and obligations that household life required. A person who could not be trusted in their business dealings was not merely guilty of a moral failing — they were a threat to the stability of the relationships their community depended upon.

It also explains why Proverbs pays significant attention to the formation of young men entering adult life. The opening chapters of the book are explicitly addressed to a son on the verge of taking on adult responsibilities — someone who must learn to navigate friendships, romantic attraction, commercial relationships, and community obligations with wisdom and integrity before the consequences of poor judgment become permanent. The urgency in the father's voice throughout these chapters reflects a genuine awareness of how much is at stake in the formation of character during early adulthood.

The Wisdom Schools and the Royal Court

Another important dimension of the world behind Proverbs involves the institutional settings in which wisdom was cultivated and transmitted. Although the household was the primary context for the transmission of practical wisdom, the book also reflects the influence of more formal educational settings — particularly the kind of scribal training associated with the royal court.

Ancient Near Eastern societies developed sophisticated administrative structures that required skilled scribes capable of reading, writing, composing documents, and advising leaders. In Israel, the royal court of Solomon and his successors maintained this kind of educated class, and the development of wisdom literature appears to have been closely connected to it. The literacy required to compose, collect, and organize the material in Proverbs points toward a setting in which writing was a practiced art — and the content of much of the book reflects the concerns of those who were being trained to advise and serve within complex social and political institutions.

This court connection helps explain some features of Proverbs that might otherwise seem surprising. The book's extensive attention to the character of a king — to what distinguishes a ruler who brings stability from one who brings ruin — reflects a context in which the quality of leadership had direct consequences for large populations. The repeated observations about the dangers of flattery, the importance of honest counsel, and the value of advisors who speak truth rather than telling powerful people what they want to hear — these were not merely ethical observations. They were practically urgent in a setting where the difference between a king who listened to honest advice and one who surrounded himself with flatterers could determine the welfare of an entire nation.

At the same time, the wisdom reflected in Proverbs was never confined to elite settings. The observations about family relationships, the raising of children, the dangers of certain kinds of companions, and the value of a hardworking and trustworthy character — these were concerns of ordinary households as much as royal courts. The book addresses both dimensions because wisdom, in its deepest understanding, is not a possession of the educated elite. It is a human capacity available to anyone willing to pursue it with appropriate humility and attention.

The Wisdom Tradition of the Ancient Near East

One of the most important aspects of the world that produced Proverbs is the broader context of wisdom literature across the ancient Near East. Israel was not the only culture in the ancient world that produced and preserved collections of practical wisdom. Egypt, Mesopotamia, and surrounding cultures all developed rich traditions of wisdom instruction that bear striking similarities to material found in Proverbs — in form, in content, and in the underlying conviction that careful observation of human behavior yields patterns of insight worth preserving and passing on.

Egyptian wisdom texts, some of which predate the biblical material by many centuries, contain instructions addressed from teachers to students on topics ranging from proper speech in the presence of superiors to the management of household resources to the dangers of associating with the wrong kind of people. Mesopotamian wisdom texts similarly preserve observations about the relationship between character, conduct, and outcome. In at least one case — a section of Proverbs that begins in chapter twenty-two — scholars have identified close parallels with a specific Egyptian wisdom text, suggesting that the sages of Israel were in conversation with the broader wisdom traditions of their world.

This international dimension of wisdom is significant for several reasons. It demonstrates that the concerns addressed in Proverbs were not merely parochial — they were recognized as genuinely human concerns across widely different cultures. It also illustrates something important about the nature of wisdom as the book understands it: because God created an ordered world, careful observation of how that world actually works yields genuine insight. The sages of Israel were not reluctant to learn from the wisdom of other cultures because they understood that all genuine wisdom ultimately reflects the order built into creation by its maker.

At the same time, the wisdom tradition of Proverbs is distinctively shaped by Israel's particular understanding of God. The fear of the Lord — the foundational orientation of the whole book — is not merely a universal religious sentiment. It is specifically the posture of humility before the God who made the world, who holds history in his hands, and whose purposes are ultimately beyond human comprehension. This distinctive foundation sets Israelite wisdom apart even as it shares formal and thematic similarities with its neighbors.

The Role of Oral Tradition

Before these sayings and poems were collected and written down, they circulated orally within the communities that produced them. A well-crafted proverb could be remembered and repeated without being written — indeed, the very qualities that make a good proverb memorable are qualities suited to oral transmission. Its compression, its rhythm, its unexpected turn of phrase, its capacity to stick in the mind after a single encounter — all of these are features of oral art as much as written literature.

This oral background left its mark on the book. The short, balanced, parallel structure of the individual proverb was not merely an aesthetic choice. It was a form designed to be carried in memory, repeated across generations, tested against experience, and taught from parent to child in the course of ordinary life. Children growing up in ancient Israel would have encountered many of these sayings long before they encountered them as part of a written collection — hearing them from parents, from elders, from neighbors whose accumulated experience gave the observations authority.

This pattern of transmission explains why Proverbs frequently emphasizes the importance of listening, of openness to instruction, and of the willingness to learn from those with more experience. In a culture where wisdom was transmitted primarily through relationship rather than institution, the disposition of the learner mattered enormously. A person who was too proud to receive correction, too impatient to observe before acting, or too attached to their own opinions to consider that they might be wrong was, by that very disposition, cutting themselves off from the accumulated wisdom of their community. The teachable person had access to resources the proud person did not — and that difference in access was, over time, a difference in the kind of person each became.

Leadership and Justice

Life in ancient Israel was also shaped by persistent questions of leadership and justice. The nation existed within a region where political power shifted frequently, where larger empires cast long shadows over smaller kingdoms, and where the quality of internal leadership had direct consequences for the welfare of ordinary people. Within this environment, the character of those in authority carried enormous practical weight.

The book of Proverbs reflects these concerns directly. A significant portion of its observations address the character and conduct of rulers — what distinguishes a king who brings stability and justice from one who brings confusion and oppression, what kinds of advisors a wise ruler seeks out, and what happens when those in positions of power abuse their authority for personal gain. These observations were not merely theoretical. They were the kind of practical wisdom that shaped the formation of those who would eventually exercise leadership within Israelite society.

At the same time, the concern for justice in Proverbs extends well beyond the conduct of rulers. The book repeatedly returns to the situation of the poor and vulnerable — to the obligation of those with resources to deal generously and fairly with those without them, and to the moral seriousness of exploiting the disadvantaged for personal gain. These concerns reflect an understanding of wisdom that is not merely self-serving. The truly wise person is not simply someone who manages their own life effectively. They are someone whose wisdom overflows into concern for others — particularly those whom the structures of society have left most exposed.

The Experience of Vulnerability

Another factor shaping the world of Proverbs was the vulnerability experienced by individuals and communities in a pre-modern world. Life in ancient Israel lacked the institutional buffers that provide stability for most people in modern societies. There were no advanced medical systems capable of addressing serious illness, no social safety nets to cushion economic misfortune, and no complex legal frameworks to protect individuals from the consequences of bad relationships or poor decisions.

In this environment, the quality of one's character and the network of relationships one had cultivated were among the most important resources available. A person who had developed a reputation for honesty, reliability, and fair dealing had built something that would serve them in times of difficulty — neighbors who would extend help, creditors who would offer flexibility, community members who would speak well of them when it mattered. A person who had built a reputation for deception, laziness, or exploitation had undermined the very relationships they might one day need most.

Proverbs reflects this awareness throughout its pages. The book's consistent attention to reputation, to the long-term consequences of character, and to the difference between what seems advantageous in the short term and what actually serves a person well over time — all of this reflects a world in which the stakes of character development were concrete and visible.

The Natural World as a Source of Reflection

One of the recurring features of Proverbs' world is the way the natural environment provides material for reflection on human life. The sages who produced this material were careful observers not only of human behavior but of the natural world — and they drew freely on what they observed in creation as a source of insight about how people should live.

The famous passage in Proverbs that directs the lazy person to observe the ant — watching how it stores food without any overseer or commander compelling it to do so — is one example of this broader habit. The natural world, for the sages of Proverbs, was not merely background scenery. It was a living display of the order built into creation by a wise God — and careful attention to that order could yield genuine insight into human life. The ant's diligence is not arbitrary. It reflects a pattern built into creation that speaks directly to human responsibility.

This observational habit also explains the broad scope of the book's attention. Proverbs notices the flight of birds, the movement of armies, the behavior of fire, the properties of water, and dozens of other natural phenomena — and in each case, what is observed in the natural world illuminates something about the shape of human wisdom or folly. The world, as Proverbs understands it, is not a neutral stage on which human life happens. It is a revelation — speaking, to those attentive enough to listen, about the nature of the God who made it and the kind of life that fits within the order He established.

Continuity and Change

Although the historical setting of Proverbs may feel distant from the modern world, the underlying human concerns that shaped the book remain deeply familiar. People today still navigate questions of how to manage resources, how to speak truthfully in relationships that matter, how to resist short-term temptations in favor of long-term good, and how to exercise whatever authority they hold with integrity rather than for personal advantage. The forms through which these challenges present themselves have changed enormously. The challenges themselves have not.

Understanding the historical world behind Proverbs does more than provide background information. It helps readers see how ancient communities approached challenges that remain recognizable today — and in doing so, it opens up the possibility of genuine learning across the distance of centuries. The sages who produced this material were not naive. They had observed life carefully and accumulated insight over generations. What they preserved was not merely a product of their time. It was a distillation of something more durable — observations about how human beings actually work, what genuinely makes life better or worse, and what kind of character enables a person to navigate complexity with integrity and purpose.

These are not ancient questions that happen to have modern echoes. They are human questions — the kind that surface in every generation, in every culture, as long as people live in a world they did not make and cannot fully control.

With this historical background in mind, we are now prepared to examine the structure and flow of the book itself. In the next chapter, we will explore how the major sections of Proverbs fit together and how the movement of the book as a whole reveals something important about its vision of the wise life.

Chapter 4

The Story or Flow of the Book

*"Listen, my son, to your father's instruction and do not forsake
your mother's teaching. They are a garland to grace your head and
a chain to adorn your neck."*
— Proverbs 1:8–9

Understanding the Structure of Proverbs

Unlike many other books of the Bible, the book of Proverbs does
not unfold as a continuous narrative. There are no central
characters whose lives develop across chapters, no sequence of
historical events building toward a climax, and no single sustained
argument moving from premise to conclusion. Instead, Proverbs
consists of a collection of sayings, instructions, and poems written
across many generations and brought together into a unified book
through a process of deliberate editorial arrangement.

Because of this, readers sometimes struggle to understand
how the book fits together as a whole. When someone first opens
Proverbs, it can appear to be a gathering of unrelated observations
placed side by side without any clear connection between them.
One verse may address the importance of honest speech, while
the next turns to the behavior of a lazy person, and the next
reflects on the character of a good ruler. The scope is wide, and
the transitions can feel abrupt.

At first glance, this variety can make the book seem
fragmentary or randomly assembled. Yet when Proverbs is
examined more carefully, a deeper structure begins to emerge. The
book does not tell a single story, but it does reflect a larger vision
shaped by people who had thought carefully about what wisdom

is, where it comes from, and how it is developed over a human lifetime.

Rather than following a storyline of events, Proverbs traces the shape of a wise life — from the initial call to pursue wisdom, through the vast accumulated observations of what wisdom looks like in practice, to the closing images of wisdom embodied in a human life. This is worth pausing on, because it reshapes how a reader might approach the book. The flow of Proverbs is not defined by chronological events. It is defined by the movement from invitation to formation to embodiment — a movement that mirrors the actual process by which any person becomes wiser over time.

As introduced in Chapter 2, the book contains several major sections with distinct characters and purposes. That structural framework is the skeleton. This chapter is concerned with the living movement within it: how Proverbs flows, how its different sections relate to one another, and what the overall shape of the collection reveals about its vision of the wise life.

Proverbs in Israel's Educational Life

The book of Proverbs was not written to sit passively on a page. It was designed to be taught, memorized, repeated, and tested against the experience of real life. Understanding how it functioned in education and formation is essential to understanding why it is arranged as it is.

Wisdom instruction in ancient Israel was not primarily an institutional activity. It happened within households, between parents and children, and in the kind of extended relationships between experienced elders and younger people that characterized community life. A father passing on what he had learned to a son about to take on adult responsibilities, a mother shaping the habits and values of the children in her care, a teacher in the royal court preparing a student for the demands of public life — these were the settings in which the material preserved in Proverbs was alive and in use.

Within these settings, the sayings and poems of Proverbs gave voice to what had been observed, tested, and found reliable across generations. They were not simply rules to be followed. They were concentrated experience — the kind of insight that can only be earned through years of careful attention, compressed into a form that could be carried and applied by someone who had not yet lived long enough to earn it themselves. The young person who internalized these teachings was not merely gaining information. They were being given a head start — access to the accumulated wisdom of people who had already navigated the challenges they were about to face.

This educational intent shapes the flow of the book in important ways. The opening section of Proverbs is not simply a preface. It is a sustained attempt to convince the reader that wisdom is worth pursuing — that its value exceeds anything else that might compete for a young person's attention and energy. Before presenting the practical observations of the central collections, the book first makes the case that those observations matter.

The educational intent of the opening chapters also explains some of their most distinctive literary features. The repeated direct address — my son, listen — is not merely a rhetorical device. It places the reader in a specific relationship: that of someone young and still forming, in the presence of someone older whose accumulated experience gives their words authority. This is not the language of a legal code or a theological treatise. It is the language of a parent speaking urgently to a child at a moment when the choices the child is about to make will shape the rest of their life.

That urgency is palpable throughout the opening chapters, and it serves a purpose. The sages who shaped this material understood something important about how wisdom is acquired:

it is not enough to simply present correct observations and expect them to take root. The learner must first be convinced that wisdom matters — that the choice between wisdom and folly is genuinely serious, genuinely consequential, and genuinely available to be made. The extended argument of the opening chapters is designed to produce that conviction before the specific observations of the central collections are encountered. A student who has been genuinely persuaded that wisdom is worth pursuing everything to obtain will engage with the material that follows very differently from one who has not.

This sequence reflects a pedagogical sophistication that is worth appreciating. The book does not assume that readers will automatically recognize the value of what it is offering. It makes the case. And the case it makes is not abstract — it is vivid, concrete, and at times almost urgent in its appeal. Wisdom is personified as a woman calling out in the streets, desperate to be heard. Folly is personified as a seductress whose house leads down to death. The stakes are presented in terms that a young person on the threshold of adult life can feel viscerally, not merely understand intellectually. That emotional engagement with the importance of wisdom is the prerequisite for genuine formation, and the opening chapters work to produce it.

From Individual Instruction to Accumulated Observation

Although the various sections of Proverbs address different audiences and use different literary forms, there is a discernible movement across the book as a whole. The opening chapters establish the framework within which everything else is meant to be understood. The great central collections then demonstrate what wisdom looks like in practice. And the closing chapters bring the book to a conclusion that is both theologically grounding and humanly specific.

The movement from the extended poems of chapters one through nine to the dense collections of short sayings in chapters ten through twenty-nine represents a shift in approach that mirrors a shift in the educational process itself. A student beginning the study of wisdom needs orientation — a sense of why this pursuit matters, what is at stake, and what wisdom actually is. The opening chapters provide exactly this. They argue at length, through poetry, personification, and direct appeal, that wisdom is the most valuable thing a person can pursue. They present the alternative — folly — with vivid clarity, making plain what is lost when the invitation to wisdom is refused.

Once that orientation has been established, the student is ready for the accumulated observations of the central collections. Here, the book shifts to a different mode entirely. Rather than an extended argument, it offers brief, compressed observation — sayings designed to be remembered, turned over in the mind, tested against experience, and deepened through repeated encounter. The transition from the opening chapters to the central collections is itself a kind of pedagogical move. Having established why wisdom matters, the book now demonstrates what it looks like in concrete, observable practice.

A Journey Through Different Dimensions of Wisdom

Although Proverbs does not follow a chronological storyline, the collection can be understood as a journey through the different dimensions of what it means to live wisely. As readers move through the book, they encounter wisdom addressed to virtually every domain of human life — the management of household resources, the cultivation of honest relationships, the exercise of authority, the treatment of the poor, the patterns of speech that build or destroy community, and the inner dispositions of character that shape all of these from the inside.

These different dimensions are not presented as separate topics between which no connection exists. They reflect a unified vision of human life in which all of these areas are expressions of the same underlying reality: the character of the person making the choices. Wisdom, in the understanding of Proverbs, is not a collection of competencies. It is a way of being — a formed character that expresses itself across every dimension of life in recognizable and consistent ways.

This is why the book moves so freely between topics that might seem unrelated to one another. The observation about honest weights in the marketplace and the observation about a gentle answer turning away wrath are not two unrelated pieces of advice. They are two expressions of the same formed character — a person who has learned to deal with others honestly and with genuine concern for their well-being. Proverbs keeps showing the reader what this character looks like from different angles, in different situations, accumulating a portrait that becomes clearer with each additional observation.

The Movement Toward Completion

One of the most significant patterns within Proverbs becomes visible only when the book is viewed as a whole. While the central collections present wisdom in its practical, observable dimensions — what it looks like in specific situations — the closing chapters of the book move toward a deeper level of reflection that brings the whole vision to completion.

The words of Agur in chapter thirty represent one of the most remarkable passages in the book — a voice acknowledging with striking humility the limits of human wisdom before the mystery of a God whose understanding exceeds all human comprehension. After hundreds of verses presenting what wisdom looks like in concrete human situations, this acknowledgment of finitude is not a contradiction. It is the deepest form of wisdom that the book has been commending all along. The fear of the Lord, which the book identified as the beginning of wisdom in its opening pages, reappears here in its most searching form — not as a starting point to be left behind, but as the posture that genuine wisdom never outgrows.

The instruction of a mother to her royal son in chapter thirty-one continues this movement toward a kind of wisdom that is both thoroughly practical and grounded in something beyond mere pragmatics. The qualities she commends in a ruler — justice toward the poor, strength of character, reliability in the exercise of power — connect the practical wisdom of the central collections with the values that have shaped the entire book.

And then the book concludes with a poem about a woman of noble character that is, in every sense, a completion. Wisdom, which was personified as a woman calling out in the streets at the beginning of the book, finds its human embodiment here at the end — not in abstract virtue, but in a specific life of diligence, generosity, wisdom in speech, and genuine care for the people around her. The poem does not describe someone who has followed a set of rules. It describes someone in whom wisdom has become character — someone whose entire way of being expresses what the book has been commending from its opening lines.

The Proverbs as a Guide for Life

In addition to their role in communal education and formation, the sayings of Proverbs have long served as guides for personal reflection and decision-making. Because the collection addresses such a wide range of human situations, many readers have found that particular proverbs speak with unusual precision to the specific challenges they face.

Throughout history, individuals have returned to the book of Proverbs during times of decision, difficulty, and reflection. The observations about speech, about the management of conflict, about the dangers of pride and the value of counsel — these touch areas of life that remain as relevant now as they were when the sayings were first composed. Someone navigating a difficult relationship may find that a particular proverb captures the dynamics of the situation more accurately than anything they could formulate themselves. Another person wrestling with the temptation to take a shortcut that seems to offer quick advantage may find in the book's repeated observations about short-term thinking a clarity that strengthens their resolve.

This ability to speak with precision into specific situations is one reason Proverbs has remained central to the wisdom traditions of communities across many centuries and cultures. The book does not offer abstract principles that must be laboriously applied to concrete situations. It offers observations about concrete situations that carry their application within themselves. A reader does not so much apply a proverb as recognize it — seeing in the saying a pattern that matches what they are experiencing and finding in that recognition both illumination and guidance.

Seeing Proverbs as a Whole

When readers first encounter the book of Proverbs, it may appear to be a loosely assembled collection of useful observations. Yet when its structure and purpose are understood, a deeper pattern becomes visible.

The movement from the extended wisdom poems of chapters one through nine, through the vast central collections, and on to the closing reflections and poems represents a coherent educational and formational arc. The book begins by making the case for wisdom, moves through the detailed demonstration of what wisdom looks like in practice, and concludes by grounding the whole vision in its ultimate source and giving it its most complete human expression.

Together, these elements show that Proverbs is more than a collection of practical tips. It is a carefully designed invitation to the lifelong pursuit of wisdom — one that is patient enough to argue, demonstrate, and embody its case rather than simply assert it.

The flow of Proverbs mirrors the movement of a life shaped by wisdom itself. The beginning is full of appeal and warning, calling the reader toward something worth pursuing with everything they have. The long middle is full of the texture of daily life — the small choices, habitual patterns, and relational realities in which wisdom is actually expressed or neglected. And the ending is full of depth and completion — a life in which wisdom has become character, and character has become a kind of praise.

The Psalter preserves moments of spiritual experience so that future readers can find language for their own. Proverbs preserves accumulated wisdom about human life so that future generations can learn from what their predecessors observed. Both are forms of gift — one reaching across time to offer vocabulary for the inner life, the other reaching across time to offer orientation for the practical one.

In the next chapter, we will examine the key themes that run throughout Proverbs — the recurring concerns and convictions that shape the book's vision of wisdom and give its diverse material a recognizable unity.

Chapter 5

Key Themes

"Trust in the Lord with all your heart and lean not on your own understanding; in all your ways submit to him, and he will make your paths straight."
— Proverbs 3:5–6

The Fear of the Lord as the Foundation of Wisdom

One of the most foundational themes running throughout the book of Proverbs is the relationship between wisdom and the fear of the Lord. This phrase appears at the very opening of the book — identified explicitly as the beginning of wisdom — and it recurs at key moments throughout the collection, functioning as the interpretive key that unlocks the meaning of everything else the book says.

The fear of the Lord is frequently misunderstood by modern readers who hear the word fear and assume the phrase describes terror or dread. In the wisdom tradition of Proverbs, the concept is considerably richer. It describes a posture of the whole person before God — an acknowledgment that God is the creator and sustainer of the world, that his wisdom exceeds human understanding, and that the appropriate human response to this reality is humility rather than self-sufficiency. A person who fears the Lord is not a person who cowers in anxiety. They are a person who has rightly understood their own place within a larger order they did not make and cannot ultimately control.

This posture has practical consequences throughout the book. The person who fears the Lord is teachable — willing to receive instruction because they recognize they do not already know everything they need to know. They are honest — because they understand that God sees what human observers miss, and that deception is ultimately futile before an all-knowing creator. They are generous — because they understand that the resources they manage are gifts held in trust rather than possessions to be hoarded. The fear of the Lord is not one theme among many in Proverbs. It is the root from which all the other themes grow.

What makes this foundation significant is that it prevents the wisdom of Proverbs from collapsing into mere pragmatism. A purely pragmatic reading of the book would suggest that its observations about honesty, diligence, and generosity are commended simply because they tend to produce good outcomes. The fear of the Lord insists on something more — that these qualities are right in themselves, because they reflect the character of a God who is himself honest, diligent in his care for creation, and inexhaustibly generous. Wisdom, in the deepest sense, is conforming one's life to the shape of reality as God has made it.

The Pursuit of Wisdom and the Danger of Folly

Closely connected with the theme of the fear of the Lord is the sustained contrast between wisdom and folly that runs throughout the book. Proverbs does not simply describe what wisdom looks like and leave it at that. It places wisdom in persistent contrast with its opposite, making clear at every turn that the choice between them is serious and its consequences real.

The opening chapters of the book dramatize this contrast through the personification of both Wisdom and Folly as women calling out to passers-by in the public spaces of the city. Wisdom builds her house, prepares her feast, and invites the simple to turn aside from their ignorance and learn. Folly also calls out — in almost identical language — offering pleasures that seem attractive but lead to destruction. The parallel between the two figures is deliberate. The invitation of folly sounds very much like the invitation of wisdom. Discerning the difference requires exactly the kind of careful judgment that wisdom itself develops.

Throughout the central collections of the book, this contrast continues in a different mode. The wise person and the fool appear repeatedly, their different habits of mind and patterns of behavior generating different outcomes over time. The wise person accepts correction and grows. The fool resists instruction and repeats the same mistakes. The wise person thinks before speaking and chooses words carefully. The fool speaks without reflection and damages relationships that take years to build. The contrast is not designed to flatter the reader by implying that wisdom is easy. It is designed to make the stakes of character formation impossible to ignore.

Speech and the Power of Words

Few themes in Proverbs receive more sustained attention than the power of human speech. The book returns to this subject repeatedly across all its major sections, from short observations about the damage done by careless words to extended reflections on what distinguishes speech that builds from speech that destroys.

Proverbs understands that what a person says reveals who they are. Speech is not merely a tool that the self uses to communicate. It is an expression of the character behind it. Honest speech comes from a person who values truth. Gentle speech comes from a person who has learned to manage their emotions and consider the impact of their words on others. Wise speech comes from a person who thinks before speaking — who understands that words, once released, cannot be recalled, and that their effects on relationships and communities can outlast the moment that produced them.

The book is equally attentive to the damage done by speech that falls short of these standards. The tongue that speaks deceit, the words that flatter rather than inform, the gossip that erodes trust within a community, the harsh response that escalates conflict when a gentle word might have resolved it — all of these appear repeatedly as examples of what folly looks like in the specific register of human communication. The attention Proverbs gives to speech reflects a deep understanding of how much of human life is shaped by language — how much trust is built or destroyed, how many relationships are formed or broken, how many communities are strengthened or undermined by the accumulated weight of what people say to and about one another.

For modern readers, this theme carries immediate relevance. The forms through which speech causes damage have multiplied in a world of instant communication and social media. The underlying observations about honesty, restraint, and the impact of words on relationships remain as precise and urgent as they were when these sayings were first composed.

What is perhaps most striking about Proverbs' treatment of speech is the depth of psychological insight it reflects. The book does not merely observe that certain kinds of speech cause damage and leave it at that. It traces the inner dynamics from which different patterns of speech emerge — the pride that produces boastful speech, the fear that produces flattery, the anger that produces harsh words, the insecurity that produces gossip. These observations suggest that the problem of speech is ultimately a problem of character, and that attempting to manage speech without addressing the character that produces it is a project that will always be working upstream.

This psychological depth gives Proverbs' observations about speech a different quality than simple etiquette advice. The book is not primarily concerned with whether a person says the right things in the right social contexts. It is concerned with whether a person has developed the kind of inner life from which genuinely good speech naturally flows — a character that is honest because it values truth, restrained because it cares about the impact of its words on others, and wise enough to know that silence is sometimes the most powerful form of speech available. That kind of character cannot be performed. It has to be formed. And Proverbs is consistently pointing its reader toward the slow, patient work of that formation rather than the quicker satisfaction of managing appearances.

Diligence, Work, and the Stewardship of Resources

Another major theme running throughout Proverbs involves the relationship between diligence and the stewardship of what one has been given. The book pays sustained attention to the habits of industry and discipline that enable a person to build something lasting — and to the patterns of laziness and poor management that slowly undermine what could have been built.

The observations about diligence in Proverbs are not simply motivational appeals to work harder. They reflect a sophisticated understanding of how character expresses itself through habits of effort and attention over time. The diligent person does not merely accomplish more than the lazy person. They develop, through the discipline of consistent effort, qualities of character — reliability, attention to detail, the ability to finish what they start — that serve them across every dimension of life. Work, in the understanding of Proverbs, is not merely instrumental. It is formative.

The book's attention to the management of resources reflects a similar depth. The observations about debt, about planning for the future, about the difference between genuine wealth and the appearance of wealth, and about the dangers of hasty decisions in financial matters — all of these reflect a community in which the consequences of poor stewardship were concrete and immediate. But they also reflect something more than practical financial wisdom. They reflect an understanding that what a person does with what they have been given reveals their character — their values, their priorities, and their orientation toward the world and other people.

There is also a social dimension to the stewardship Proverbs commends that is easy to overlook when the book's observations about work and resources are read primarily as individual guidance. The sages consistently understood responsible stewardship as having consequences beyond the individual — as something that either strengthens or weakens the community that depends on the reliability and integrity of its members. A person who manages their resources poorly does not merely harm themselves. They become less capable of contributing to the broader network of mutual support and obligation that sustains community life. A person who manages them well becomes a resource for others — someone whose stability and reliability create conditions in which the people around them can also flourish.

This communal dimension transforms the book's observations about diligence and stewardship from mere personal finance advice into something with explicitly moral weight. Being trustworthy with what one has been given is not simply a strategy for personal prosperity. It is a form of service — an expression of the kind of character that takes seriously its responsibilities to the people and community it is part of.

Justice, Generosity, and the Poor

Another theme that recurs throughout the book of Proverbs with striking consistency is the moral obligation to deal justly and generously with those who are vulnerable. The book returns repeatedly to the situation of the poor — to the responsibility of those with resources to treat them with fairness and dignity, and to the moral seriousness of exploiting or ignoring those who have been left most exposed by the structures of society.

This concern is not peripheral to the wisdom tradition of Proverbs. It is central. The book consistently links the treatment of the poor with the fear of the Lord — noting that whoever mocks the poor shows contempt for their maker, and that whoever is kind to the needy honors God. The connection is direct and unambiguous: how a person treats the most vulnerable members of their community is not a peripheral ethical concern. It is an expression of whether they have genuinely understood who God is and what he cares about.

Proverbs also addresses justice in commercial relationships — the use of honest weights and measures, the avoidance of fraud, and the expectation that those who hold positions of power will exercise them for the benefit of the community rather than for personal gain. These concerns reflect the everyday economic realities of ancient Israelite life, but they articulate a vision of justice that extends far beyond any particular cultural setting. The insistence that every person deserves to be dealt with honestly and fairly — regardless of their social position or ability to protect their own interests — is one of the most consistently recurring convictions in the entire book.

The Shape of Relationships

The final major theme that runs throughout Proverbs is the quality and character of human relationships. The book pays extensive attention to friendship, marriage, family, and the various kinds of relationships through which people are shaped for better or worse over the course of their lives.

Proverbs understands that human beings are formed by the company they keep. The repeated warnings about the kinds of companions who lead toward destruction — those whose habits of deception, violence, or moral carelessness are contagious — reflect an acute awareness of how much influence the people closest to us exercise over the people we become. The corresponding commendation of friendships characterized by honesty, loyalty, and genuine concern for the other's well-being reflects an equally acute awareness of how much such relationships can support and sustain the pursuit of wisdom.

The book's attention to marriage reflects a similar depth. The extended descriptions of both the wisdom and folly that can characterize domestic life make clear that the household is understood as a formative environment — one in which wisdom is either cultivated or undermined by the quality of the central relationship at its heart. The closing poem of the book, describing a woman of noble character, is the fullest expression of this theme: a portrait of someone in whom wisdom has become character, and whose relationships — with her household, her community, and the wider world — are the expression of that formed character in action.

Themes That Intertwine

When the themes of the fear of the Lord, the pursuit of wisdom, speech, diligence, justice, and relationships are considered together, they reveal how Proverbs operates as an interconnected work rather than a random collection of observations. Each theme appears repeatedly across the book's different sections, reinforcing the others and deepening the overall vision of what a wise life looks like.

The fear of the Lord is the root from which all the other themes grow. The pursuit of wisdom is the sustained activity it generates. Speech, diligence, justice, and relationships are the domains in which that wisdom is expressed and tested in the concrete texture of daily life. None of these themes operates in isolation. A person's speech reflects their character, which is shaped by their relationships, which are governed by their sense of justice, which is grounded in their fear of the Lord. The themes are not separate chapters in the same book — they are woven through every page.

Together, these themes form the foundation of Proverbs' enduring relevance. The book does not attempt to simplify the complexities of human life. Instead, it acknowledges those complexities while directing attention toward a vision of wisdom that encompasses every dimension of what it means to live well. Understanding these themes prepares readers to engage Proverbs more deeply — recognizing not just what any individual saying is observing, but how it participates in the larger conversation about wisdom that the book as a whole has been sustaining across centuries.

In the next chapter, we will examine how readers sometimes misunderstand Proverbs when they approach the book without considering its historical and literary context. Recognizing these common misunderstandings helps clarify how the book is intended to function and what it is actually trying to do.

Chapter 6

Where People Get It Wrong

"The way of fools seems right to them, but the wise listen to advice."
— *Proverbs 12:15*

Treating Proverbs as Guaranteed Promises

One of the most common and consequential misunderstandings readers bring to the book of Proverbs is the assumption that its sayings function as unconditional promises — that if a person follows the teaching of the book, they can expect specific, predictable outcomes in return. This reading treats Proverbs as a kind of contractual arrangement: do this, and that will follow. Raise your children correctly, and they will never go astray. Work diligently, and you will become wealthy. Speak honestly, and relationships will flourish. Act justly, and justice will come back to you.

The problem with this reading is not that the observations in Proverbs are false. Most of them reflect genuine patterns in human experience — patterns that are real and worth attending to. The problem is that Proverbs is describing tendencies, not guarantees. A proverb captures how things generally work, not how they always work without exception. The book itself, read carefully and as a whole, is aware of this. The closing chapters include voices that acknowledge the limits of human wisdom and the mystery of God's purposes in ways that prevent the earlier observations from hardening into a formula.

Treating proverbs as promises leads to predictable difficulties. A parent who has done everything right watches a child make destructive choices and concludes that the book has failed them

— or worse, that they have failed in some hidden way they cannot identify. A diligent person who loses their livelihood through no fault of their own feels accused by the book's observations about the fruits of hard work. A righteous person who faces unjust suffering concludes either that they must have done something wrong or that the book is simply not true.

None of these conclusions is warranted. They arise from a category error — reading a book of wisdom observations as though it were a book of binding guarantees. Proverbs is offering the reader the accumulated insight of people who have paid careful attention to how life works. That insight is genuinely valuable. But it is not a formula that overrides the complexity and unpredictability of actual human experience.

Reading Individual Proverbs Without Context

A second common misunderstanding arises when readers approach Proverbs as a collection of isolated sayings, each complete in itself, without attending to the context provided by the surrounding material or the book as a whole. This reading treats the book as a sourcebook for quotations — a place to find a useful saying for a particular situation — rather than as a coherent work with a sustained vision of wisdom.

The difficulty with this approach is that it can lead to misapplication. A proverb read in isolation, without the interpretive framework provided by the opening chapters or the awareness of how the book's different sections relate to one another, is more likely to be applied mechanically than wisely. The book itself is explicit about this risk — it knows that the same observation can be true in one situation and misleading in another, and it expects its reader to develop the judgment to tell the difference.

This is precisely why the opening chapters of Proverbs are so important. They do not simply present useful sayings. They attempt to form a certain kind of reader — one who understands what wisdom is, where it comes from, and what is required to actually develop it. A reader who skips the opening section and goes directly to the central collections is like a student who ignores the foundational instruction and tries to apply advanced techniques they have not yet understood. The observations may be accurate, but the wisdom to apply them well has not yet been developed.

Reading Proverbs well means reading it as a whole — allowing the framework of the opening chapters to shape how the individual sayings of the central collections are understood and allowing the closing chapters to deepen and qualify the vision that has been built up along the way.

Ignoring the Book's Internal Tensions

A third misunderstanding occurs when readers smooth over the apparent tensions and contradictions within the book rather than engaging with them seriously. Proverbs contains sayings that seem, at first glance, to point in opposite directions. Do not answer a fool according to his folly, one verse says — and two verses later, answer a fool according to his folly. The juxtaposition is jarring if a reader expects the book to provide consistent, universally applicable rules.

But this tension is not a mistake. It is a teaching. The book is not telling the reader which of these two approaches is correct. It is telling the reader that both are sometimes correct — and that wisdom consists in knowing which one applies in a given situation. That kind of contextual judgment cannot be reduced to a rule. It has to be developed through experience, observation, and the kind of careful attention that the book is trying to cultivate.

Readers who are troubled by these internal tensions are often revealing an expectation that Proverbs does not share — the expectation that wisdom can be reduced to a consistent algorithm. The book resists that expectation deliberately. It knows that life is more complex than any fixed formula can capture, and it is trying to develop in its reader a mind flexible and perceptive enough to navigate that complexity rather than a mind that has simply memorized the right answers.

Engaging seriously with the tensions in Proverbs is itself a formative practice. It requires the reader to think carefully, to consider multiple perspectives, and to resist the temptation of premature certainty. These are precisely the habits of mind that the book is trying to develop.

Expecting Proverbs to Offer Emotional Comfort

A misunderstanding that often accompanies the others involves approaching Proverbs primarily as a source of comfort or reassurance. Readers familiar with other parts of the Bible — particularly the Psalms, with their rich vocabulary of lament, trust, and consolation — sometimes bring similar expectations to Proverbs and are surprised to find a book that is more demanding than comforting, more diagnostic than consoling.

Proverbs is not primarily a book of comfort. It is a book of formation. Its purpose is not to make the reader feel better about their current situation. It is to make the reader wiser, which sometimes requires the uncomfortable recognition that one's current patterns of thought or behavior are part of the problem one is trying to solve. The book's observations about pride, laziness, careless speech, and the unwillingness to receive correction are not offered as gentle encouragements. They are offered as accurate diagnoses — and diagnoses are only useful if they are received honestly rather than deflected.

This does not mean that Proverbs contains no comfort. The repeated affirmations that wisdom is available, that God gives it generously to those who seek it, and that the righteous life leads toward genuine flourishing rather than mere appearance — these are genuinely encouraging. But the comfort they offer is of a different kind from the emotional consolation of the Psalms. It is the comfort of clarity — the reassurance that comes from understanding one's situation accurately and knowing the direction one ought to move.

Treating the Book as Primarily About Financial Success

Another misunderstanding that shapes how some readers approach Proverbs involves the assumption that the book is primarily about material prosperity — that its core promise is financial security in exchange for diligence and right behavior. This reading is understandable given the prominence of economic themes in the book, but it fundamentally misrepresents what Proverbs is actually commending.

The wealth that Proverbs values is not primarily financial. The book consistently emphasizes that a good name is worth more than great riches, that wisdom and understanding are more valuable than gold and silver, and that the person who gains wealth through dishonesty has gained nothing worth having. The diligence Proverbs commends is not merely a strategy for accumulating resources. It is an expression of character — of the kind of person who takes their responsibilities seriously and does what they undertake with care and attention.

When Proverbs associates diligence with prosperity, it is not offering a formula for wealth. It is observing a genuine pattern — that people who apply themselves consistently, manage their resources wisely, and maintain their integrity in economic dealings tend to build something durable over time. That observation is true as a general tendency. It is not a guarantee, and it is not the main point. The main point is the character that produces the diligence, not the prosperity the diligence may produce.

Readers who approach Proverbs as a guide to financial success will miss the book's deeper and more important concern — the formation of a person whose entire way of being reflects wisdom, integrity, and genuine care for others.

Reading the Wisdom as Purely Human Achievement

A misunderstanding that cuts close to the theological center of the book involves reading its wisdom as a purely human achievement — as though the accumulated observations of careful people were simply a body of practical knowledge that any thoughtful person could develop through their own efforts, independent of any relationship with God.

This reading entirely misses the significance of the fear of the Lord as the book's foundational theme. Proverbs is not presenting wisdom as something that begins with human observation and arrives at God as a conclusion. It is presenting wisdom as something that begins with God — with a right orientation toward the creator of the ordered world, whose wisdom is embedded in the fabric of reality — and flows from there into every dimension of practical life.

This distinction matters enormously for how the book is read. A reader who approaches Proverbs as a collection of humanly derived practical insights will treat it as advice — useful, perhaps even compelling, but ultimately optional and subject to revision based on their own experience and judgment. A reader who understands the fear of the Lord as the beginning of wisdom will approach the book differently — as a guide to understanding a reality that exists independently of their own preferences and that makes claims on their life regardless of whether they find those claims convenient.

The humility that the book commends throughout is not merely strategic. It is a recognition that human beings are not the measure of all things — that there is a larger wisdom built into creation that exceeds human comprehension, and that the posture of openness and teachability before that wisdom is the condition for genuinely learning anything at all.

Overlooking the Book's Emotional Register

A misunderstanding that is less commonly identified but practically significant involves overlooking the emotional register in which much of Proverbs is written. The book is sometimes approached as a purely rational document — a collection of logical observations about cause and effect in human behavior. In this reading, Proverbs is primarily a book of good advice, commending wise choices because they produce better outcomes than foolish ones.

But the opening chapters are written in a register that is considerably warmer and more urgent than mere rational counsel. The voice of the parent calling to the son is not the voice of a dispassionate advisor presenting options. It is the voice of someone who genuinely loves the person they are addressing and is deeply concerned about what will happen to them if they do not listen. The personification of wisdom as a woman calling out in the streets — desperate to be heard, grieved when she is ignored — gives the invitation to wisdom an emotional intensity that pure logic cannot produce. And the description of the consequences of refusing wisdom, rendered in the vivid imagery of a path that descends toward death, is designed to create not merely understanding but felt conviction.

This emotional register is part of the book's pedagogical design. The sages understood that genuine motivation to pursue wisdom requires more than intellectual assent to its value. It requires something felt — a sense of the stakes that is visceral as well as rational. Proverbs is not merely trying to inform its readers. It is trying to move them — to create a genuine desire for wisdom and a genuine aversion to folly that will hold up under the pressure of specific temptations when they arrive. Readers who flatten the emotional register of the book by treating it as a purely rational document are missing one of its most important formative tools.

Misunderstanding the Closing Poem

Many readers either overlook or misread the closing poem of Proverbs — the extended description of a woman of noble character that concludes the book. Some read it as a domestic ideal directed specifically at women, relevant only to those managing a household. Others read it as an unrealistic standard that sets an impossibly demanding vision of female virtue. Both readings miss what the poem is actually doing within the structure of the book.

The closing poem is a completion. Throughout the book, wisdom has been personified as a woman — calling out in the streets, building her house, inviting the simple to come and learn. The closing poem answers that personification with a human embodiment. Here, at the end of the book, is what wisdom looks like when it has become character in a real human life — not in the abstract, not as an ideal, but as a specific pattern of diligence, generosity, honesty in speech, and genuine care for the people around her.

The poem is addressed to everyone who has read the book — not only to women, and not only to those who manage households. It is a portrait of what the wise life looks like in practice, rendered in vivid and specific human terms. The qualities it describes — reliability, careful attention to responsibilities, generous concern for the vulnerable, wisdom in speech, and a life grounded in the fear of the Lord — are the same qualities the book has been commending throughout. The poem simply shows what they look like when they have been fully integrated into a human life.

The Proverbs as Formation

When these common misunderstandings are addressed, the actual
purpose of Proverbs becomes considerably clearer. The book is
not primarily a collection of practical tips, financial advice, or
religious encouragements. It is a carefully designed instrument of
formation — a body of instruction, observation, and poetic
artistry designed to develop in its reader the kind of mind and
character that wisdom requires.

The variety of literary forms within the book — extended
argument, compressed observation, personification, poem,
dramatic contrast — is not accidental. Each form does something
that the others cannot. The extended argument of the opening
chapters persuades. The compressed observations of the central
collections train habits of perception. The dramatic contrast
between wisdom and folly sharpens judgment. The closing poem
gives the whole vision a human face. Together they constitute not
a textbook but an education — one that operates on the reader at
multiple levels simultaneously.

This formative role helps explain why Proverbs has remained
central to communities of faith across many centuries and
cultures. Its usefulness is not exhausted by a single reading.
Communities have returned to these observations again and again
because the formation they offer is never complete — wisdom is
always being developed, never fully arrived at, and the book meets
readers at every stage of that development with something they
had not yet seen.

Learning to Read Proverbs Thoughtfully

Approaching Proverbs thoughtfully involves a few simple but
important habits. Reading each saying within the context provided
by its surrounding material — rather than lifting it in isolation —
reveals layers of meaning that isolated reading misses. Attending

to the book's overall structure, and particularly to the framework established by the opening chapters, provides the interpretive lens through which the central collections are best understood. Sitting with the book's apparent tensions rather than resolving them too quickly develops the contextual judgment that wisdom actually requires. And reading the closing chapters not as an afterthought but as the completion they are gives the whole book the ending it has been building toward.

None of this requires scholarly expertise. It requires only the willingness to read carefully, to return to the same material more than once, and to ask not just what a particular saying means but what kind of person reading it is meant to form. Proverbs rewards that kind of attention generously. The reader who brings patience and humility to the book will find that it offers far more than the reader who approaches it only as a sourcebook for useful phrases — though it will sometimes offer that too, precisely because the insights it preserves are grounded in careful observation of how human life actually works.

In the next chapter, we will explore how the themes and insights of Proverbs continue to speak into modern life. Although the world in which these sayings were composed differs enormously from the present, the questions they address remain deeply relevant for readers today.

Chapter 7

What It Means for Modern Life

*"The beginning of wisdom is this: Get wisdom. Though it cost all
you have, get understanding."*
— Proverbs 4:7

Ancient Observations in a Modern World

When modern readers approach the book of Proverbs, they often
find it surprisingly accessible — more immediately recognizable
than many other parts of the Bible. The sayings address situations
that feel familiar: the difficulty of controlling one's temper, the
damage done by gossip, the slow consequences of laziness, and
the value of honest counsel. Unlike the historical narratives or
prophetic literature of the Old Testament, Proverbs seems to
speak directly to the texture of daily life without requiring
extensive background knowledge.

Yet this accessibility can itself become a barrier. Because
Proverbs feels familiar, readers sometimes assume they have
understood it more quickly than they actually have — extracting a
handful of useful observations, nodding at their practical wisdom,
and moving on without engaging the deeper vision the book is
commending. The surface accessibility of Proverbs conceals a
depth that only extended and thoughtful engagement reveals.

The reason this depth remains relevant is the same reason it
was relevant when these sayings were first composed. The external
circumstances of life have changed dramatically — the cultural
setting, the economic arrangements, the social structures within
which people navigate their relationships and responsibilities are
all very different from the ancient Near Eastern world that
produced Proverbs. But the internal challenges that shape human

life have not changed at all. People still struggle with pride and its costs. They still face the temptation to take shortcuts that seem advantageous in the short term and prove destructive over time. They still find that the quality of their relationships depends heavily on the quality of their speech, their reliability, and the genuineness of their concern for others.

This chapter examines what that relevance looks like in practice: how Proverbs changes the way modern readers approach character formation, decision-making, relationships, and the question of what a good life actually consists of. Not what the book meant in the ancient world — that has been the work of earlier chapters — but what it makes possible today.

The Formation of Character in a Culture of Performance

One of the most practically urgent gifts Proverbs offers modern readers is its sustained insistence on the priority of character over performance. Contemporary culture is deeply shaped by metrics of achievement and external appearance — by résumés, social media profiles, productivity measures, and the various forms of impression management that technology has made both easier and more demanding. The pressure to appear successful, competent, and well-adjusted is pervasive, and it operates even in domains — like personal relationships and spiritual life — where it arguably has no place.

Proverbs is entirely uninterested in performance. The book consistently redirects attention from external appearance to internal reality — from what a person seems to be to what they actually are. The person who appears wealthy but has achieved that appearance through dishonesty is, in the book's estimation, poor in the ways that actually matter. The person who appears confident but whose confidence rests on unwillingness to receive correction is, by that very confidence, cut off from the growth that genuine wisdom requires. The person who appears religious but whose concern for the poor is absent has failed to understand the most basic implication of the fear of the Lord.

For modern readers, this reorientation is practically valuable and personally demanding. It asks a different set of questions than those that contemporary culture tends to pose. Not how am I appearing, but who am I actually becoming. Not what am I achieving, but what kind of person are my habitual choices forming me into. Not how am I presenting myself to others, but what would the accumulated pattern of my daily decisions reveal to anyone who could see them clearly. These are not comfortable questions, but they are the right ones — and Proverbs has been asking them with unusual persistence for a very long time.

Wisdom and the Management of Speech

The theme of speech in Proverbs carries immediate and practical relevance for modern readers navigating a world in which words travel faster, reach further, and persist longer than at any previous point in human history. The ancient sages who observed that the tongue has the power of life and death could not have anticipated the specific forms through which that observation would become more, not less, true in the twenty-first century. But the underlying insight — that what we say shapes what we are and affects the people around us in ways that often outlast the moment of speaking — has not diminished.

Proverbs is exceptionally practical on this subject. The book does not merely observe that careless speech causes damage. It identifies the specific patterns — flattery that deceives, gossip that erodes trust, harsh words that escalate conflict, proud speech that forecloses the possibility of learning — and it describes their consequences in ways that are recognizable to anyone who has experienced them. The person who has watched a community fractured by gossip, a relationship damaged by a thoughtless comment, or a conflict escalated by a harsh response will find that Proverbs has been there before and has something precise to say about it.

The practical application is not merely to speak less, though restraint has its place. It is to develop the kind of character from which good speech naturally flows — a character that values truth enough to be honest even when honesty is uncomfortable, that cares enough about the people it speaks to and about to choose words that serve rather than wound, and that has enough self-awareness to recognize when silence is wiser than speech. These are habits that can be developed, and Proverbs suggests that developing them is one of the most practically significant investments a person can make.

The Question of What Makes Life Good

One of the places where Proverbs speaks most directly to the concerns of modern readers is in its sustained engagement with the question of what makes a life genuinely good — as opposed to merely successful, comfortable, or well-regarded. Contemporary culture offers many answers to this question, and they tend to cluster around acquisition: of wealth, of status, of experiences, of the various markers that signal to others and to oneself that life is going well. Proverbs is skeptical of all of them.

The book consistently distinguishes between what seems good and what actually is good — and the gap between these two is one of its central preoccupations. A proverb that captures this in compact form observes that there is a way that appears right to a person, but its end is the way of death. The observation is stark, but it is not pessimistic. It is a call to the kind of careful, honest evaluation of one's own choices and values that prevents the slow drift toward something one would not have chosen if one had seen it clearly.

What Proverbs ultimately commends as the good life is not spectacular. It does not promise great wealth, extraordinary achievement, or the admiration of large numbers of people. It commends a life characterized by honesty in relationships, diligence in one's responsibilities, genuine concern for the vulnerable, wisdom in speech, and an orientation toward God that keeps all of these in their right perspective. This vision is available to anyone — it does not depend on exceptional talent, favorable circumstances, or social advantage. It depends on character, and character is the one thing that every person has the ability to develop regardless of what else they have been given.

Navigating Complexity Without Certainty

Another practical gift Proverbs offers modern readers is its approach to decision-making in the absence of certainty. Contemporary life presents people with an almost overwhelming array of choices — about careers, relationships, investments, values, and the countless smaller decisions that accumulate into the shape of a life. The cultural pressure is often to find the correct answer, the optimal choice, the best possible outcome — and the anxiety produced by the awareness that one cannot always know which choice that is can be considerable.

Proverbs does not promise certainty. What it offers instead is something more useful: a way of thinking about decisions that tends to lead toward better outcomes over time, even in the absence of guaranteed results. The book's counsel to seek multiple advisors, to resist the seductiveness of shortcuts, to think carefully about the long-term character consequences of near-term choices, and to maintain the humility to recognize the limits of one's own understanding — these are not algorithms that produce correct answers. They are habits of mind that improve the quality of decision-making across a wide range of situations.

For modern readers, this approach is both realistic and practical. It does not promise that following wisdom will prevent all bad outcomes — Proverbs itself is too honest about the complexity of life to make that claim. It promises that cultivating the habits of mind the book commends will make a person more capable of navigating complexity wisely — better equipped to learn from experience, more resistant to the specific forms of self-deception that reliably produce poor decisions, and more genuinely attentive to the interests of others as well as their own.

Wisdom and the Inner Life

One of the dimensions of Proverbs that carries perhaps the most distinctive relevance for modern readers is its sustained attention to the inner life — to what goes on inside a person beneath the level of observable behavior. Contemporary culture pays considerable attention to external behavior, particularly in professional and public contexts. It pays considerably less attention to the inner dispositions, habits of thought, and emotional patterns from which that behavior flows. Proverbs is consistently interested in both — and it consistently insists that the inner life is the more important of the two.

The book's concern with what it calls the heart — the deep center of a person's thought, desire, and motivation — runs throughout its pages. Proverbs understands that the heart is not merely the location of emotion. It is the source from which all of a person's observable behavior ultimately flows. The words a person speaks reflect what is in their heart. The decisions they make under pressure reveal what their heart actually values, as opposed to what they claim to value when the cost of their values is low. The patterns of behavior they fall into when no one of consequence is watching express the actual condition of their heart with a clarity that carefully managed public behavior often conceals.

This means that the formation Proverbs is pursuing goes deeper than behavior modification. The book is not satisfied with a person who does the right things for the wrong reasons — who acts honestly out of fear of consequences rather than genuine commitment to truth, or who is generous in observable situations while remaining fundamentally indifferent to the well-being of others. It is reaching toward a transformation of the inner life itself — a genuine change in what a person loves, values, and desires — from which genuinely good behavior will then flow naturally rather than being maintained through effort.

For modern readers navigating a culture that is saturated with external metrics and public performance, this attention to the inner life is both a corrective and a relief. It is a corrective because it insists that the question of who one is actually becoming — in one's habits of thought, in the disposition of one's attention, in the actual condition of one's values and desires — matters more than the question of how one appears. It is a relief because it points toward a kind of integrity that does not require constant management — a life in which the outer and the inner are genuinely aligned, and the effort required to maintain the appearance of virtue is no longer necessary because the virtue itself has been formed.

Proverbs describes this condition not as an impossible ideal but as the natural outcome of the wisdom the book has been commending throughout — a life in which the fear of the Lord has so thoroughly shaped the inner life that its outward expressions are genuine rather than performed. That is the destination the book has been pointing toward from its opening invitation, and it is the most practically important thing it has to offer the modern reader who is willing to receive it.

Justice and Generosity in Everyday Life

The modern world is marked by persistent questions about inequality, fairness, and the obligations that those with resources have toward those without them. Whether in public conversations about economic structures or in the more immediate questions that arise in ordinary life about how to treat the people one actually encounters, the concern for justice and generosity remains as urgent now as it was when these sayings were first composed.

Proverbs engages these concerns in ways that are both direct and practical. The book does not approach justice as primarily a structural or political question — though it does not ignore the structural dimensions of how communities treat their most vulnerable members. It approaches justice primarily as a matter of character — of the habits of attention, generosity, and honest dealing that each person develops and expresses in the specific relationships and responsibilities that make up their daily life.

For modern readers, this grounding in character rather than ideology is practically useful. It places the question of justice within the reach of ordinary people, making ordinary decisions — how do I treat the people I actually encounter, what do I do with the resources I actually have, how do I exercise whatever authority I actually hold? These are not questions that require large-scale structural change before they can be answered. They are questions that every person can engage with in the texture of their daily life, and Proverbs insists that how they are answered matters enormously — both for the people affected and for the character of the person answering them.

The Examined Life as a Daily Practice

One of the most practical implications of Proverbs' vision of wisdom is that it transforms the ordinary rhythms of daily life into opportunities for formation. The book does not reserve its attention for the large, defining decisions that arrive at significant turning points — the major career choice, the significant relationship commitment, the high-stakes ethical dilemma. It attends equally, and perhaps more persistently, to the small and ordinary: the daily habits of speech, the routine management of responsibilities, the habitual patterns of response to frustration, and the quiet daily choices about how one treats the people immediately around them.

This attention to the ordinary is not incidental. It reflects an understanding of how character actually forms — not primarily through dramatic moments of decision, but through the slow accumulation of small choices made in unremarkable circumstances. The person who practices honesty in low-stakes situations is developing the character that will hold in high-stakes ones. The person who treats the people immediately around them with genuine care and attention is forming the habits of attention that will extend, over time, to a wider circle of concern. The person who manages small responsibilities reliably is building the kind of trustworthiness that eventually becomes a defining feature of who they are.

Proverbs implies throughout its pages that wisdom is therefore not primarily a Sunday practice or an occasional exercise. It is woven into the texture of every day — present in how a person begins their morning, how they manage the conflicts and frustrations that arrive without warning, how they speak to the people they see so regularly that those people have become invisible, and how they end the day with an honest accounting of how they actually lived it. The examined life that wisdom requires is not a life of constant self-scrutiny or anxious self-monitoring. It is a life in which the habits of honest self-awareness have been developed to the point where seeing oneself clearly has become natural rather than threatening.

For modern readers, this daily dimension of wisdom is both demanding and accessible. It is demanding because it removes the comfortable assumption that wisdom is something achieved in significant moments and then maintained at a low cost in between. It is accessible because it means that the pursuit of wisdom does not require exceptional circumstances or unusual opportunities. It requires only the willingness to bring genuine attention to what is already present — the relationships, responsibilities, and situations that make up the ordinary fabric of daily life — and to engage with them as the formative material they actually are.

Proverbs has been saying this, in various ways and from various angles, across all of its pages. The sages who produced this material were not writing for people whose lives were particularly dramatic or whose challenges were unusually complex. They were writing for people who got up in the morning and faced a day full of ordinary interactions and ordinary decisions — the same kind of day that most people face most of the time. The wisdom they preserved was designed for exactly that kind of day. And it is in exactly that kind of day that the formation they were seeking to produce either happens or does not.

That is perhaps the most practically useful thing Proverbs has to say to the modern reader: that the life they are already living is the material from which wisdom is built. Not a different life, not a simpler or more dramatic one, but this one — with its specific relationships, specific responsibilities, specific frustrations and satisfactions and recurring temptations. The invitation the book extends is not to leave that life behind and pursue something more elevated. It is to inhabit the life one already has with greater honesty, greater care, and greater attention to what is actually being formed through the choices one makes within it day by day.

The reader who accepts that invitation will not arrive at a destination where wisdom is finally complete, and the work of formation is done. Proverbs does not promise that endpoint. What it promises is something more honest and more valuable: that the person who pursues wisdom seriously, day by day, across the ordinary circumstances of a real life, will become someone different than they would have been — someone whose character has been genuinely shaped, whose relationships have genuinely deepened, and whose ability to navigate the complexity of life with integrity and discernment has genuinely grown. That is what wisdom produces. And Proverbs has always insisted that it is worth everything required to pursue it.

A Living Tradition

The continued influence of Proverbs across centuries demonstrates that these observations have become part of a living tradition — one that has never stopped being used and never stopped finding new readers who recognize the accuracy of its observations about human life. Communities have returned to these sayings in moments of decision, formation, and reflection, discovering that the accumulated wisdom of people who paid careful attention to how life actually works has not been superseded by the passage of time.

This ongoing engagement is itself a practical argument for the book. Proverbs has been tested across an enormous range of human circumstances — wealthy societies and poor ones, stable political environments and chaotic ones, periods of religious confidence and periods of deep uncertainty. The same observations have continued to serve all of these situations because they are not primarily observations about external circumstances. They are observations about human nature, human character, and the persistent patterns of choice and consequence that shape human lives regardless of when or where those lives are lived.

As individuals encounter Proverbs today, they join a long line of readers who have turned to these writings for guidance, formation, and the kind of practical clarity that comes from encountering an observation that is simply and undeniably true. That track record is not incidental. It is part of what Proverbs is

— a body of wisdom that has proven durable precisely because it was grounded, from the beginning, in careful attention to what is actually real.

Chapter 8

Modern Reflection

"Above all else, guard your heart, for everything you do flows from it."
— Proverbs 4:23

What Proverbs Does to the Reader

The previous chapter examined what modern readers can do with Proverbs — how its observations can be applied as practical resources for navigating character formation, decision-making, relationships, and the question of what makes a life genuinely good. This chapter is concerned with a different question: what Proverbs does to the reader. Not the immediate application of a saying to a specific situation, but the slower, less visible work that happens when a person engages with the book seriously and repeatedly over time.

The distinction matters because Proverbs was never only about providing useful observations for specific situations. It was designed to form people — to shape the habits of mind and perception through which individuals see the world, evaluate their own choices, and orient themselves toward what actually matters. That kind of formation does not happen in a single reading. It accumulates across years of return, across different seasons of life, across the gradual process of allowing a particular kind of attentiveness and reflection to become one's own.

The opening chapters of Proverbs set this expectation from the start. The person wisdom calls out to is not someone who needs a quick answer to an immediate question. It is someone who has not yet developed the habits of mind that wisdom requires — someone who needs not just information but formation. The call is not to consult the book when needed and set it aside. It is to inhabit a particular kind of attention to life, sustained over time, until it becomes the natural way of seeing. That is the posture Proverbs is ultimately designed to cultivate, and it is the posture this chapter explores.

The Rhythm of Observation and Return

Formation through Proverbs begins with a particular kind of reading — one that is willing to return to the same material from different angles and different seasons of life, and to find that the same observations mean something different depending on where one is standing when one encounters them. This is not a coincidence or a limitation of the book. It is how the wisdom tradition was designed to work.

A proverb encountered at twenty carries one meaning. Encountered at forty, after a specific experience that the saying seemed to predict, it carries another. Encountered at sixty, looking back across a life, it may carry a third — both confirmation and something more complex, a recognition that the pattern the saying described was real but that its implications were deeper than originally understood. The book does not change. The reader changes. And because the reader changes, the encounter with the same material keeps producing new understanding.

This quality of accumulating meaning over time is not something a reader can force. It requires the willingness to return — to treat the book not as something to be read once and understood but as something to be lived alongside, consulted at different stages of life, and allowed to speak into circumstances that the reader could not have anticipated when they first encountered it. Formation through Proverbs is partly the slow development of that willingness — learning to trust that returning to what seems familiar will consistently reveal something that was not visible before.

Attention and the Reshaping of Perception

The deeper challenge of modern life is not simply that it moves too fast, though it does. The deeper challenge is that the pace and structure of modern life shapes how people think — training them to respond quickly, to prefer immediate clarity over patient observation, and to treat the kind of slow, sustained attention that genuine understanding requires as a luxury rather than a necessity. The habits of mind that contemporary culture tends to reinforce are habits of surface engagement: identify, categorize, respond, move on.

Proverbs interrupts this pattern. The book does not merely ask readers to slow down. It models a different relationship to experience altogether — one characterized by careful observation, patient attention to patterns that only become visible over time, and the willingness to sit with complexity rather than resolving it prematurely. The sages who produced this material were not people in a hurry. They were people who had paid careful attention to how human life actually works across long stretches of time — and what they preserved reflects that quality of attention.

Readers who engage with Proverbs regularly over time often find that this practice begins to transfer. The habit of observing before acting, of looking for the pattern beneath the surface event, of asking not just what is happening but what it reveals about the character of the people involved and the dynamics at work — this becomes a way of moving through the world. Not because readers are consciously imitating the sages, but because sustained encounter with that kind of attentive reflection gradually reshapes how observation happens.

This is the distinction between information and formation. Information tells readers something. Formation changes how they see. Proverbs is not primarily informational — it does not communicate a set of facts to be retained and applied. It is formative — it models a way of attending to experience that, over time, becomes the reader's own way of attending to it. That is what the opening chapters are reaching toward when they call not merely for compliance with wisdom's instructions but for the love of wisdom itself — not someone who has read the book, but someone who has been changed by sustained engagement with it.

The Slow Development of Judgment

One of the practices Proverbs models most consistently — and one that shapes readers most durably over time — is the development of contextual judgment. The book does not simply present observations to be memorized and applied. It presents observations alongside their qualifications, exceptions alongside their rules, and apparent contradictions alongside their resolutions — and it expects the reader to develop, through sustained engagement, the ability to navigate all of this with genuine discernment rather than mechanical application.

This development of judgment is not something that can be rushed. It requires exposure to a wide range of situations, the willingness to apply what has been learned and observe the results, the honesty to acknowledge when an approach that seemed right produced the wrong outcome, and the humility to revise one's understanding accordingly. Proverbs models this kind of learning across its many voices and many sections — showing wisdom from enough different angles that no single perspective can be taken as the whole picture.

Readers who stay with Proverbs over time absorb this orientation. They learn it not by studying it abstractly but by encountering it repeatedly across the book, in different sayings and different contexts, until the instinct to look for the qualification, to ask about the exception, to resist the mechanical application of any single principle, becomes a natural feature of how they think. When a new situation arises, the habit of asking not just what rule applies but what the situation actually requires — what specific form of wisdom this particular set of circumstances calls for — becomes available because it has been modeled so consistently.

The sages also practiced this development of judgment in a communal dimension, drawing not only on individual experience but on the inherited observations of many people across many generations. A person facing a situation they have never personally navigated can still reach back to what others observed and find in that record a source of orientation. This accumulated wisdom carries a particular resonance for modern readers who feel that their own experience is too limited to provide reliable guidance. Proverbs invites them into a longer tradition. They do not need to figure everything out from scratch. Others have gone before, and their careful observations still speak.

A Voice for the Examined Life

Beneath the specific practices Proverbs models — careful observation, patient attention, contextual judgment — there is something more fundamental that sustained engagement with the book cultivates: a particular orientation toward one's own life. A habit of examination. The willingness to ask not just what one is doing but what kind of person one is becoming through what one does — to treat the question of character not as a background concern that can be deferred but as the central concern that shapes everything else.

This orientation does not come naturally in a culture that emphasizes external achievement over internal formation. Contemporary life provides countless metrics for evaluating how one is performing — in career, in relationships, in health, in social standing. It provides relatively few frameworks for the more important question of who one is actually becoming through the accumulated pattern of one's choices. Proverbs insists on that question persistently, from many angles, across many subjects. The effect of sustained engagement with it is the gradual development of a self-awareness that is not self-absorbed but genuinely useful — the ability to see one's own patterns clearly enough to evaluate them honestly and change what needs to change.

What Proverbs offers is not resolution so much as orientation. The sages have been in the same places — the places of temptation, of pride, of the seductive short-term advantage that proves destructive over time, of the relationship that could have been deepened if the right words had been chosen. They have observed the same patterns and recorded what they found. Yet they have continued — to observe, to reflect, to pass on what they learned. That continuation is itself part of what Proverbs communicates. To keep attending, to keep examining, to keep bringing one's own life into honest relationship with what wisdom has to say about human life in general — that is the posture the book models from its opening invitation to its closing poem. Formation through Proverbs is, in the end, the slow acquisition of that posture.

Continuing the Conversation

To read Proverbs seriously is to step into something already in motion. These observations have been carried across centuries, taught and repeated in settings of family formation, communal education, and personal reflection. They have shaped how individuals and communities understand the relationship between character and conduct — not by telling people what to conclude but by demonstrating, again and again, what careful attention to human life reveals.

There is something worth pausing on in the sheer durability of that tradition. These sayings have been returned to in circumstances as varied as human history itself — in periods of stability and in times of upheaval, in moments of personal confidence and in the depths of individual confusion. They have been passed from parents to children in ordinary households and preserved in the libraries of the learned. They have accompanied decisions of enormous consequence and the small daily choices that, accumulated over time, determine the kind of person one becomes. The fact that the same observations have continued to serve such an enormous range of human situations is not incidental. It points to something in Proverbs that operates at a level deeper than any single circumstance — a quality that transcends the specific and speaks to the enduring.

For the modern reader, this means that engaging seriously with Proverbs is not an exercise in recovering something that once mattered but no longer does. It is an encounter with a living body of wisdom that has never stopped being used, never stopped being returned to, never stopped finding new readers who recognize the accuracy of its observations about their own lives. The conversation the sages began has not concluded. Each person who reads these observations with genuine attention and allows them to shape how they see themselves and the world becomes part of that ongoing exchange — not as a passive recipient, but as someone whose own experience now enters into dialogue with the accumulated wisdom the book preserves.

The invitation is not simply to understand Proverbs from the outside. It is to allow it to do what it has always done — to meet readers where they actually are, to give shape to what they are beginning to see about themselves and the world, and to draw that recognition into the larger conversation about what it means to live wisely, honestly, and with genuine care for the people and responsibilities one has been given. That is what Proverbs has always been for. And that is what it remains.

Chapter 9

Reflection Questions

"Let the wise listen and add to their learning, and let the discerning get guidance — for understanding proverbs and parables, the sayings and riddles of the wise."
— Proverbs 1:5–6

The book of Proverbs invites readers into a sustained engagement with some of the most persistent questions of human life. Rather than presenting a rigid system of rules or a guaranteed formula for success, the book offers accumulated observations drawn from careful attention to how human beings actually live — what builds character over time, what erodes it, what makes relationships trustworthy, what makes them destructive, and what it means to move through the complexity of daily life with genuine wisdom and integrity.

Because of this, engaging with Proverbs often raises questions that lead readers into deeper reflection about their own lives. The sages who produced this material were not merely describing other people. They were describing patterns that appear in every person's experience — the temptation to take the easy path, the consequences of careless speech, the slow formation that happens through habitual choices made day after day. Their observations invite readers to participate in the same kind of honest self-examination.

For many people, Proverbs becomes most meaningful when it is approached not simply as ancient wisdom but as a mirror — something that reflects back a recognizable image of one's own habits, patterns, and tendencies. The qualities it commends and the failures it identifies remain part of human experience today. That continuity is not accidental. It reflects the fact that the questions the sages were addressing are the same questions that surface in every generation, regardless of how different the surrounding world may look.

The following questions are designed to help readers reflect on how the themes of Proverbs connect with their own lives. Some focus on the character qualities the book commends, while others explore broader ideas related to wisdom, speech, relationships, justice, and the nature of a good life. They are not intended to produce simple answers. Instead, they encourage thoughtful engagement with the text and invite readers to consider how the insights of Proverbs might influence their understanding of themselves and their responsibilities.

These questions can be approached individually or discussed within a group setting. Either approach allows space for the ideas found within Proverbs to take root through careful consideration. There is value in both — private reflection tends to surface personal connections that might not emerge in conversation, while group discussion often introduces perspectives that an individual reader would not have reached alone. Proverbs itself models both modes: some of its observations feel like private counsel whispered between a parent and child, others like observations about human nature that are simply and undeniably true for anyone paying attention.

When readers pause to consider the themes within these sayings, they often begin to recognize how the observations of the sages connect with their own experience. That recognition is frequently where the most meaningful engagement begins.

1. The Fear of the Lord and Genuine Humility

One of the most foundational themes in Proverbs is the relationship between wisdom and the fear of the Lord. The book identifies this posture — an acknowledgment of God's authority, wisdom, and the limits of human understanding — as the beginning of wisdom rather than a conclusion one arrives at after having become wise. This sequence matters. Humility before God is not the reward for wisdom. It is the condition that makes wisdom possible.

This theme challenges a common modern assumption: that confidence and self-sufficiency are virtues to be cultivated, and that the acknowledgment of one's own limits is a form of weakness. Proverbs consistently inverts this assumption, observing that pride is one of the most reliable predictors of eventual failure, while the humility that remains genuinely open to correction and instruction is one of the most reliable preconditions for growth.

Reflect on the following questions:

- In what areas of your life do you find it most difficult to remain genuinely open to correction or instruction?
- How does the fear of the Lord as described in Proverbs differ from the way humility is typically understood in contemporary culture?
- What would it look like practically for the fear of the Lord to function as the beginning — rather than the conclusion — of one's pursuit of wisdom?
- Can you identify a time when pride or overconfidence led you toward a decision you later recognized as poor?
- What practices or habits help you remain teachable as you move through different seasons of life?

Proverbs demonstrates that genuine humility is not a passive quality. It is an active orientation — a deliberate refusal to overestimate one's own understanding, a willingness to listen before speaking, and a consistent acknowledgment that the complexity of life exceeds any individual's ability to fully grasp it. Far from being a weakness, this orientation is, in the book's understanding, the most accurate response to reality that a human being can have — and it is the posture from which all genuine wisdom grows.

2. Speech and Its Consequences

Few themes in Proverbs receive more sustained attention than the power of human speech. The book returns to this subject repeatedly across all its major sections, and its observations touch situations that every reader will recognize — the word spoken in anger that cannot be taken back, the flattery that felt like encouragement but was actually manipulation, the gossip that seemed harmless until relationships began to erode, the honest word spoken at the right moment that changed everything.

Proverbs understands that what a person says is not separable from who they are. Speech reveals character — it exposes what someone actually values, how they actually think about other people, and what they are actually trying to accomplish in their relationships. The book's consistent attention to speech is not a surface-level concern with etiquette. It is a deep concern with the kind of person one is becoming, visible in nothing so clearly as in the words one habitually chooses.

Consider the following questions:

- In what kinds of situations do you find it most difficult to choose your words carefully?

- What difference do you notice in your relationships when you speak with greater honesty and care versus when you speak carelessly?

- Can you identify patterns in your own speech — tendencies toward flattery, harsh criticism, or deflection — that Proverbs might identify as worth examining?

- What would it look like to take the book's observations about speech seriously as a practical discipline over the next month?

- How does the speed and scale of modern communication — text messages, social media, email — change the stakes of careless speech in ways the ancient sages could not have anticipated?

86

The Psalms demonstrate that language shapes reality — that the words we choose in our relationships have consequences that outlast the moment of speaking. Proverbs insists on the same truth with particular force. The reader who takes this seriously is not merely trying to avoid saying the wrong thing. They are developing a character from which genuinely good speech naturally flows — a character that values honesty enough to be truthful even when truth is uncomfortable, and values others enough to speak in ways that serve rather than harm.

3. Diligence and the Management of Responsibility

Proverbs pays sustained attention to the habits of diligence and responsible stewardship — to the difference between the person who applies themselves consistently and the person who avoids the demands of their responsibilities. These observations can feel moralistic if read in isolation, but in context they reflect something more interesting: a careful attention to how character expresses itself through habitual patterns of effort and avoidance, and how those patterns compound over time.

The book is not primarily interested in productivity. It is interested in the kind of person who, when given a responsibility, can be trusted to take it seriously — not because they are being watched, but because their character has been formed in a way that takes responsibility seriously for its own sake. That kind of reliability, the sages observed, is built slowly through habits of attention and follow-through, and it is undermined just as slowly by habits of avoidance and excuse.

Consider the following questions:

- In what areas of your life do you find it most tempting to avoid or defer the responsibilities you have taken on?
- What is the difference between the diligence Proverbs commends and the kind of relentless productivity that contemporary culture sometimes promotes?

- How do the habits you practice in small, everyday responsibilities shape who you become in larger ones?
- Can you identify a pattern in your life where consistent small efforts have produced something durable over time?
- What does it mean to be genuinely trustworthy in the specific responsibilities you currently hold?

Proverbs suggests that the management of responsibility is not merely a practical matter. It is a character matter — one that reveals what a person actually values and what kind of person they are becoming through their habitual choices. The reader who takes this seriously is not simply trying to become more productive. They are investing in the formation of a character that can be genuinely relied upon — by the people who depend on them, by the community they are part of, and ultimately by themselves.

4. Relationships and the Company We Keep

Proverbs understands that human beings are shaped by the company they keep — that the people closest to us influence who we become in ways that are both pervasive and often invisible to us in the moment. The book pays careful attention to the kinds of relationships that support the development of wisdom and integrity, and to the kinds that gradually undermine it.

This concern is not simply about avoiding bad influences, though that is part of it. It reflects a deeper understanding of how character is formed through relationship — how the values, habits, and patterns of the people around us seep into our own thinking and behavior over time, often without our noticing. The person who chooses their closest relationships wisely is not being antisocial. They are taking seriously one of the most significant influences on the person they will eventually become.

Consider these questions:

- What qualities do you look for in the people you choose to spend most of your time with?

- Have you noticed the influence — positive or negative — that particular relationships have had on your own habits of thought and behavior over time?

- In what ways does the community you belong to shape your understanding of what matters and how to live?

- What does Proverbs suggest about the difference between genuine friendship and the kind of association that flatters without genuinely caring?

- How do you navigate relationships in which you care about someone whose patterns of behavior Proverbs would identify as harmful?

Proverbs reminds readers that relationships are not neutral. Every significant relationship either supports or gradually erodes the pursuit of wisdom — and the accumulation of those relationships, over time, is one of the most significant factors shaping the kind of person one becomes. Taking this seriously is not a call to withdraw from difficult people. It is a call to be genuinely attentive to the long-term formative influence of the relationships one chooses to invest in most deeply.

5. Justice, Generosity, and the Vulnerable

Throughout Proverbs, the treatment of the poor and vulnerable appears not as a peripheral ethical concern but as a direct expression of one's relationship to God. The book is insistent on this connection — the person who exploits the poor shows contempt for their maker, while the person who is generous toward the needy honors God. The moral weight of how we treat the most vulnerable people around us is not negotiable in Proverbs' vision of wisdom.

This concern is concrete rather than abstract. Proverbs does not address justice primarily as a political or structural question, though the book does observe what happens when those in positions of power use that power for exploitation rather than service. It addresses justice as a matter of character — of the specific habits of attention, generosity, and honest dealing that each person develops and expresses in their daily life.

Consider the following questions:

- In your daily life, who are the people most likely to be treated unjustly or overlooked, and what specific habits of attention might help you notice them?

- What is the difference between the generosity Proverbs commends and the kind of charity that maintains comfortable distance?

- How does the book's insistence that care for the poor is an expression of the fear of the Lord change how you think about generosity?

- In what ways do the economic habits you practice — how you negotiate, what you pay people for their work, how you handle situations where you have more power than the other person — reflect the kind of character Proverbs is commending or cautioning against?

- What would it look like to take Proverbs' concern for justice seriously as a practical orientation in the specific context of your life?

Proverbs demonstrates that justice is not something that happens elsewhere, in institutions and systems beyond individual influence. It happens in the specific encounters and transactions that make up daily life — in how one treats the person who has less power, less resource, and less ability to protect their own interests. The reader who takes this seriously is not simply trying to be a good person. They are developing a character whose fundamental orientation toward others reflects the generosity and fairness that the fear of the Lord requires.

6. Wisdom and the Long View

One of the most consistent features of Proverbs' approach to decision-making is its insistence on the long view — its repeated attention to the difference between what seems advantageous in the short term and what actually serves a person's genuine interests over time. The book is full of observations about shortcuts that prove destructive, gains that turn out not to be gains, and apparent advantages that come at costs that only become visible later.

This long-view orientation is one of the most practically relevant features of the book for modern readers living in a culture that consistently rewards immediate results and struggles with deferred consequences. The habits of thinking that Proverbs commends — taking seriously the long-term character consequences of near-term choices, resisting the seductiveness of the easy path, maintaining integrity even when dishonesty would produce short-term benefit — are habits that run against the grain of much contemporary culture.

Consider these questions:

- Can you identify a decision in your own experience where taking the short-term advantage produced consequences you wish you had avoided?
- What practices help you resist the pull of immediate gratification in favor of longer-term good?
- How does the book's emphasis on character over outcomes change how you evaluate the choices available to you in a particular situation?
- In what areas of your life do you find the long view most difficult to maintain?
- What does Proverbs suggest about how to build the kind of character that consistently chooses the path of wisdom even when the alternative is immediately attractive?

The enduring relevance of Proverbs' long-view orientation suggests that certain features of human nature remain consistent across generations. The seductiveness of the easy path, the temptation to prioritize appearance over reality, the pull of immediate advantage over long-term integrity — these are not modern problems. They are human problems, and the sages who observed them carefully thousands of years ago had something precise and useful to say about how to navigate them.

7. The Search for Wisdom

Throughout Proverbs, wisdom is presented not as a static possession but as something actively pursued — a way of being in the world that is developed through sustained effort, genuine humility, and the willingness to keep learning across every season of life. The book does not promise that wisdom arrives at a point where further growth becomes unnecessary. It models a posture of perpetual openness — the recognition that there is always more to understand, always a dimension of any situation that one has not yet fully seen.

This orientation toward wisdom as a lifelong pursuit rather than a finished achievement is one of the most practically important features of the book. A person who believes they have arrived at wisdom is, by that very belief, closing off the possibility of further growth. A person who maintains genuine openness — who remains curious, teachable, and honest about the limits of their own understanding — is positioning themselves to keep developing in ways that the self-satisfied person cannot.

Consider the following questions:

- What does it mean to you personally to pursue wisdom as an ongoing practice rather than a destination to be reached?

- In what areas of your life do you feel most genuinely open to continued growth, and in what areas do you notice resistance to further change?
- How does the book's vision of wisdom as a lifelong pursuit connect with your own experience of how understanding develops over time?
- What specific practices help you remain genuinely teachable as you move through different seasons of life?
- In what ways might engaging with the book of Proverbs over the coming year — returning to it in different circumstances and from different stages of your own development — produce insights that a single reading cannot?

Proverbs demonstrates that the pursuit of wisdom is itself a form of worship — an acknowledgment that there is always more to understand, always a way in which one's current grasp of reality is incomplete, and always the possibility of growth for the person who remains genuinely open to it. That openness is the posture of the fear of the Lord expressed in the domain of the mind — a recognition that wisdom ultimately belongs to God, and that human beings participate in it only as they remain humble enough to keep receiving it.

Continuing the Reflection

These questions represent only a starting point for engaging with the themes found in Proverbs. Each reader will encounter the book from a unique perspective shaped by personal experience, cultural background, and the specific responsibilities and relationships that define their current season of life. What surfaces for one reader may not surface for another, and that diversity of response is not a problem to be resolved but a reflection of the breadth of the book itself.

As individuals reflect on Proverbs, new insights often emerge over time. A saying that once seemed self-evident may later reveal its depth during a specific experience that the observation seemed to predict. A passage that once felt distant may take on new significance during a season of difficulty or decision. Questions that once felt settled may reopen. The book accommodates all of these movements because it was never intended to be encountered once and set aside.

In this way, Proverbs continues to function as a living body of wisdom that speaks across generations. By returning to these observations again and again — in different circumstances, from different stages of one's own development — readers participate in a conversation that has unfolded for thousands of years. A conversation that invites each generation to engage honestly with the enduring questions of character, wisdom, justice, and what it actually means to live well — and to bring their own experience into that ongoing exchange.

Chapter 10

Five Lessons

"Wisdom has built her house; she has set up its seven pillars. She has prepared her meat and mixed her wine; she has also set her table."
— Proverbs 9:1–2

The book of Proverbs contains a remarkable body of accumulated wisdom shaped by the careful observation of human life across many generations. These sayings and poems were composed in different historical periods and reflect a wide range of concerns, yet they share a common purpose that continues to resonate with readers today. Some passages address the management of practical responsibilities. Others explore the dynamics of relationships, the nature of honest speech, or the character qualities that distinguish a wise person from a foolish one. Still others probe the deeper questions of what wisdom actually is, where it comes from, and what it requires of those who pursue it.

Despite this diversity, several themes appear repeatedly throughout the collection. When these themes are examined together, they reveal enduring insights about the nature of wisdom, the formation of character, and the ways individuals can cultivate the kind of life that Proverbs consistently commends — not as a guaranteed formula, but as a genuine and achievable vision of what human life is capable of becoming.

The lessons that emerge from Proverbs are not presented as rigid rules or abstract theories. Instead, they appear through the accumulated observations of people who paid careful attention to how life actually works — what builds character over time, what erodes it, what kinds of choices prove genuinely good, and what kinds prove destructive regardless of how attractive they appeared at the outset. Their words provide guidance not by eliminating life's complexity, but by equipping readers to navigate that complexity with greater wisdom and integrity.

The following five lessons highlight some of the most important insights that arise from Proverbs. While each reader may discover additional themes within the book, these lessons provide a helpful framework for understanding why these observations have remained meaningful across centuries — and what they continue to offer to anyone willing to engage with them seriously.

1. Wisdom Begins With the Right Posture

One of the most foundational lessons of the book of Proverbs is that wisdom does not begin with intelligence, talent, or accumulated experience. It begins with posture — specifically, with the fear of the Lord that the book identifies from its very first pages as the beginning of wisdom and the foundation from which everything else follows.

This lesson runs against a deeply ingrained modern assumption: that wisdom is fundamentally a human achievement, arrived at through careful observation and rigorous thought. Proverbs does not deny the value of observation and thought — the book is built on them. But it insists that observation and thought, however careful and rigorous, will ultimately lead the self-sufficient person astray if they are not conducted within the framework of genuine humility before God. The person who trusts entirely in their own understanding is, in the book's estimation, the most dangerous kind of fool — not despite their intelligence, but in part because of it.

The practical implications of this lesson are considerable. A person who approaches their own life, their relationships, and their responsibilities with genuine humility — who remains teachable, who acknowledges the limits of their own perspective, who takes seriously the possibility that what seems right to them may not actually be right — is positioned to keep learning and growing in ways that the self-assured person is not. Pride, in the understanding of Proverbs, does not merely risk individual failure. It actively closes off the possibility of the growth that wisdom requires.

For modern readers, this lesson challenges the premium that contemporary culture places on confidence, self-sufficiency, and the public projection of competence. Proverbs is not opposed to confidence that is genuinely earned. It is opposed to the kind of confidence that substitutes for genuine self-awareness — the confidence that prevents a person from noticing when they are wrong, from receiving correction, and from remaining genuinely open to continued learning. The fear of the Lord is the antidote to that kind of confidence, and Proverbs insists that no amount of intelligence or experience can substitute for it.

This is also worth noting: the fear of the Lord, as Proverbs presents it, is not a burdensome obligation. It is described as a spring of life, as something that adds length of days, as the foundation of a life that is genuinely good. The humility it cultivates is not self-diminishment. It is accurate self-knowledge — and accurate self-knowledge, practiced over time, is one of the most liberating things a person can develop.

2. Character Is Formed Through Habitual Choices

A second major lesson that emerges from Proverbs is that character is not fixed. It is formed — shaped gradually through the accumulation of habitual choices made day after day, in situations large and small, in the ordinary texture of daily life where no one is particularly paying attention. The sages who produced this material understood something that modern psychology has confirmed at length: who a person is at any given moment is largely the product of who they have been choosing to become through their habitual patterns of thought and behavior over time.

This lesson has two sides. On one hand, it is genuinely encouraging. It means that wisdom is available to anyone who is willing to pursue it seriously — not as a gift reserved for the particularly intelligent or naturally virtuous, but as a quality that can be developed through sustained effort, genuine humility, and the willingness to learn from both instruction and experience. The person who begins to take seriously the formation of their character, at whatever stage of life they find themselves, is genuinely beginning something that will produce real results over time.

On the other hand, it is sobering. It means that the small choices made in ordinary moments — the impulse toward honesty or deception in a low-stakes situation, the habit of treating the people around one with care or indifference, the pattern of responding to criticism with genuine openness or defensive dismissal — are not insignificant. They are the building materials from which character is constructed. And character, once constructed, is not easily dismantled. The sages consistently observe that the habits formed in youth tend to persist throughout life — not because change is impossible, but because patterns that have been reinforced over many years develop a momentum that is genuinely difficult to reverse.

For modern readers, this lesson is both a motivation and a warning. The motivation is clear: it is always worth investing in the formation of character, because the investment compounds over time in ways that eventually produce something genuinely valuable. The warning is equally clear: the small choices made now are not inconsequential simply because their consequences are not yet visible. They are the invisible architecture of the person one is becoming — and Proverbs insists that attending to that architecture is one of the most important things any person can do.

3. Wisdom Is Expressed in Relationship

A third lesson that appears repeatedly throughout Proverbs is that wisdom is not primarily a private achievement. It is expressed in relationship — in the specific quality of how one treats the people around them, speaks to them and about them, keeps or breaks faith with them, and responds to their needs and vulnerabilities. The person whose wisdom never reaches the texture of their daily relationships is not, in the understanding of this book, genuinely wise.

This relational dimension of wisdom runs throughout every section of the book. The observations about honest speech, about faithfulness in friendship, about the treatment of those who are most vulnerable, about the quality of care brought to the closest relationships of household and family — all of these reflect an understanding of wisdom that is fundamentally oriented toward others. The wise person is not merely the person who makes good decisions for themselves. They are the person whose character makes the lives of the people around them better.

The book is particularly attentive to what happens in close relationships under pressure — when honesty becomes inconvenient, when generosity requires genuine sacrifice, when faithfulness costs something. These are the moments in which character is most clearly revealed, and Proverbs returns to them repeatedly because they are the moments in which the difference between genuine wisdom and its counterfeit is most visible. The person who is honest only when honesty is easy, generous only when generosity is convenient, and faithful only when faithfulness costs nothing has not yet developed the character the book is commending. They have developed a performance of it.

For modern readers, this lesson is a consistent reminder that the pursuit of wisdom is not a solitary project. It is worked out in relationship — in the daily encounters and interactions that either develop or erode the relational qualities that genuine wisdom requires. The reader who takes this seriously will find that some of the most important measures of their own development as a wise person are not the decisions they make in isolation, but the quality of presence, honesty, and care they bring to the people who are actually in their life.

4. The Long View Is Essential

One of the most practically significant lessons in Proverbs is the consistent insistence on the importance of the long view — on the difference between what seems advantageous in the immediate moment and what actually serves a person's genuine interests over time. The book is full of observations about this gap, and it returns to it from so many angles that its importance can hardly be missed by anyone reading with genuine attention.

The sages observed with considerable precision the specific forms that short-term thinking typically takes. The shortcut that seems to save time but builds a reputation for unreliability. The dishonest gain that seems to provide advantage but erodes the trust that makes genuine prosperity possible over time. The harsh word spoken in the heat of a moment that seems satisfying but damages a relationship that took years to build. The avoidance of a difficult responsibility that provides temporary relief but allows the underlying problem to grow until it becomes genuinely unmanageable. In each case, the short-term calculation is comprehensible — it just happens to be wrong about what actually matters.

The long view that Proverbs commends is not merely strategic patience — the calculation that waiting will eventually produce a better payoff. It is something deeper: a genuine reorientation of values that places character, integrity, and the quality of one's relationships above any short-term advantage that might be gained by compromising them. The person who has internalized this reorientation does not merely calculate that honesty pays off in the long run. They value honesty as part of the kind of person they want to be — and that valuing produces a consistency of behavior that no strategic calculation can sustain.

For modern readers navigating a culture that consistently rewards speed, immediate results, and the appearance of success over the substance of it, this lesson is both countercultural and practically urgent. The habits of character that Proverbs commends — the willingness to do the slow, patient work of building genuine trustworthiness, of developing skills and relationships that take years to mature, of maintaining integrity even when circumstances make deception easy — are investments whose returns are not always immediately visible but whose absence eventually is.

5. Wisdom Is Available, and Its Pursuit Is Worth Everything

The final and perhaps most encouraging lesson of Proverbs is that wisdom is not an esoteric possession reserved for the specially gifted or the religiously exceptional. It is available. The opening chapters of the book present wisdom as actively seeking those who will receive it — calling out in public spaces, setting her table, inviting the simple to come and learn. The book's persistent message is not that wisdom is difficult to find but that it is so often refused — and that the refusal, not the lack of access, is the tragedy.

This lesson carries with it an implicit challenge: if wisdom is available, and if its pursuit is as valuable as the book consistently claims — more valuable than silver, more precious than rubies, worth giving up everything else to obtain — then the most important question is not whether one can become wiser but whether one is genuinely willing to pursue it. The sages were clear-eyed about the obstacles. Pride resists instruction. Laziness defers the effort that growth requires. The seductive appeal of short-term pleasure diverts attention from the slower satisfactions of genuine formation. The comfortable habits of thought and behavior resist disruption even when they are producing poor results.

What Proverbs offers, against all of these obstacles, is a vision of what is possible — a vision of the wise life as something genuinely achievable, genuinely worthwhile, and genuinely available to anyone who will take its invitation seriously. The closing poem of the book gives that vision a human face: a specific life of diligence, generosity, wisdom in speech, and care for others, grounded in the fear of the Lord, that has become the embodiment of everything the book has been commending. That life is not presented as exceptional. It is presented as the natural outcome of the wisdom that the book has been inviting its reader toward from the very first page.

For readers today, this lesson is both a challenge and an encouragement. The challenge is genuine: wisdom requires something. It requires humility, sustained effort, the willingness to be corrected, and the long-term commitment to character over performance. The encouragement is equally genuine: the investment is worth it. The person who pursues wisdom seriously over time is building something that will serve them, their relationships, and their community in ways that no other investment can match. Proverbs has been saying this for thousands of years — and the durability of that message is itself part of the evidence for its truth.

The Enduring Wisdom of Proverbs

Taken together, these five lessons reveal why Proverbs continues to speak to readers today. The book captures the complexity of human experience while pointing toward a way of living that is both genuinely achievable and genuinely worth pursuing. The sages demonstrate that wisdom can include humility, careful formation, relational investment, long-term thinking, and the sustained pursuit of something more valuable than any short-term alternative. Their reflections invite readers to approach their own lives with the same seriousness and openness.

What the five lessons share is a common resistance to simplification. None of them offers a formula. None of them promises that applying the right approach will produce a predictable result in every situation. Instead, they describe a way of inhabiting life — with greater humility, more careful attention, deeper relational investment, longer perspective, and more genuine commitment to what actually matters — that the sages found sustainable and valuable across many different kinds of circumstances.

In doing so, Proverbs continues to offer guidance not through rigid answers but through a model of thoughtful formation that remains relevant in every generation. The book does not exhaust itself on a single reading. It rewards return. And the reader who returns to it across different seasons of life — bringing new experiences, new questions, and new awareness of how much there is still to learn — will find that the conversation it opens is one of the most worthwhile they have ever entered.

Continuing the Conversation

One of the most remarkable aspects of Proverbs is the way it continues to invite participation from each new generation of readers. The sages who composed and collected these observations could not have imagined the countless individuals who would later encounter their words across different cultures and centuries. Yet the observations they preserved remain recognizable today — not because the world has stayed the same, but because human nature has not changed as much as the world around it.

When readers engage with Proverbs, they enter into a conversation that stretches across history. They encounter voices that speak from another era yet still address concerns that remain deeply familiar. This conversation allows readers to explore their own lives through the lens of wisdom accumulated across generations — to test the book's observations against their own experience, to find in its precision a confirmation of what they have half-noticed themselves, and to receive from its accumulated insight a form of guidance that no single lifetime of experience could have produced.

The Psalms do not demand that readers adopt a particular interpretation or reach immediate conclusions. Neither does Proverbs. Both books create space for thoughtful engagement over time. Each reader may find that certain passages resonate more strongly depending on the circumstances of their life. Over time, the same saying may reveal new dimensions of meaning as experience deepens and the reader's capacity to understand what they are observing grows. The book does not exhaust itself on a single reading. It rewards return.

A Book That Endures

The lasting influence of Proverbs can be seen in the way its observations have been woven into the thought and practice of countless communities throughout history. Its sayings have been passed from parents to children, taught in schools and communities of faith, tested against experience in every kind of human circumstance, and consistently found to describe something real and important about how human life actually works. They have accompanied people through decisions of enormous consequence and through the small daily choices that accumulate, over time, into the shape of a life.

This enduring presence demonstrates that Proverbs speaks to something fundamental about human experience. The book acknowledges the complexity and unpredictability of life while continuing to insist that character matters, that choices have consequences, and that the habits of mind and behavior a person develops over time will shape the kind of person they ultimately become. It holds out, with remarkable persistence and consistency, a vision of the wise life as something genuinely available — not despite the difficulty of the pursuit, but through it.

For modern readers, Proverbs offers a reminder that the formation of character is not an optional supplement to the more important business of life. It is the most important business of life — the work from which everything else flows. The sages were not people who had arrived at wisdom and were reporting back from a comfortable distance. They were people in the middle of their lives, paying attention to what they saw, and choosing to pass on what they had learned. That choice — repeated across generations, preserved in the book we still hold in our hands — is what Proverbs ultimately is.

By returning to these ancient observations, readers join a long tradition of people who have sought wisdom and found in this book something that rewarded their search. The conversation that began centuries ago continues today, inviting each generation to engage seriously with the enduring wisdom found within Proverbs — and to discover, as every generation before them has discovered, that it has something genuinely worth saying.

Closing Reflection

The book of Proverbs stands as one of the most enduring collections of practical wisdom in human history. Across centuries and cultures, its sayings and poems have been read, taught, and returned to by individuals and communities seeking guidance for the ordinary and extraordinary challenges of life. From ancient households to modern classrooms, from private moments of decision to the formation of entire communities, Proverbs has remained a consistent presence within the wisdom traditions of people who have found, generation after generation, that its observations about human life remain accurate.

What gives Proverbs its lasting influence is not merely the cleverness of its sayings or the literary artistry through which they are expressed. Its enduring power lies in the accuracy with which it describes how human beings actually work — what builds character over time and what erodes it, what makes relationships trustworthy and what destroys that trust, what habits of mind consistently lead toward the kinds of outcomes people genuinely want and what habits consistently lead away from them. Within this collection, readers encounter observations that feel not simply old but true — the kind of truth that has been tested against experience across many generations and has continued to hold.

The sages who produced this material were not theorists working from comfortable distance. They were careful observers of actual human life, shaped by the same pressures, temptations, and relational complexities that shape human life in every era.

Their observations reflect what they actually saw — and what they saw has not changed as much as the world around it. The specific circumstances through which pride displays itself have shifted. The underlying dynamics of pride have not. The particular forms through which careless speech damages relationships have multiplied with the development of new communication technologies. The fundamental reality that words have consequences beyond the moment of speaking has not changed at all.

For modern readers, this continuity is both an invitation and a challenge. The invitation is to engage seriously with a body of wisdom that has been refined across centuries and that speaks with unusual precision to the specific challenges of character formation, relational integrity, and practical decision-making that every person faces. The challenge is to receive that wisdom with the genuine humility the book consistently identifies as its prerequisite — to approach Proverbs not as a reservoir of quotable encouragements but as a serious engagement with the question of who one is becoming through the accumulated pattern of one's daily choices.

In this way, Proverbs challenges assumptions that contemporary culture tends to reinforce. The modern world is deeply invested in outcomes — in what people achieve, produce, and demonstrate. Proverbs is deeply invested in character — in who people are actually becoming through the choices they make when no one of particular importance is watching. The book insists, with remarkable consistency across all its different sections and voices, that character is the foundation from which everything else flows — and that investing in its formation is the most important work any person can do.

This perspective allows Proverbs to remain meaningful for readers across generations. Although the cultural world that produced the book differs enormously from modern society, the inner dynamics it describes remain familiar. People today continue to encounter the temptation to take the easy path, the pull of short-term advantage over long-term good, the difficulty of speaking honestly when deception would be convenient, and the slow realization that the quality of one's relationships depends heavily on the quality of one's character. These are not ancient problems with modern echoes. They are human problems, as present now as they were when the sages first recorded their observations about them.

What this book has attempted to do is clear the path to that encounter. Understanding where Proverbs came from — the historical and cultural world that shaped it, the structure that organizes its diverse sections into a coherent whole, the literary forms through which it communicates — removes barriers that can otherwise keep modern readers at a distance from the material. When Proverbs is approached only as a sourcebook for useful quotations, its depth remains largely inaccessible. When it is understood as a carefully designed instrument of formation — one that argues, demonstrates, and finally embodies its vision of wisdom in a human life — it begins to reveal dimensions that casual reading cannot reach.

Each of the themes examined in this book — the fear of the Lord as the foundation of wisdom, the sustained contrast between wisdom and folly, the priority of character over performance, the long view over short-term advantage, the relational expression of wisdom in daily life — points toward the same underlying reality. Proverbs was never meant to be encountered passively. It was written to engage its reader, to challenge their assumptions, to develop their capacity for judgment, and to form the kind of person who can navigate the complexity of life with genuine wisdom and integrity. That is what it has done for generation after generation, and it is what it continues to do.

Proverbs also models something that modern readers often find difficult: the willingness to sit with complexity rather than resolving it prematurely, to develop judgment through sustained engagement rather than acquiring correct answers through a single reading, and to remain genuinely open to continued learning regardless of how much one already knows. The sages who produced this material were themselves people who had not finished learning. Their observations are offered not as final conclusions but as invitations to the same kind of careful, humble, sustained attention to life that produced them. The reader who accepts that invitation is not merely gaining information. They are being formed — gradually, across many encounters and many seasons — into someone who sees the world with greater clarity and navigates it with greater wisdom.

That formation is perhaps what Proverbs commends most consistently. Not a particular set of correct behaviors. Not a guaranteed formula for successful outcomes. But a posture — one that remains genuinely humble before what it does not yet understand, genuinely attentive to the patterns that careful observation reveals, and genuinely committed to the slow, patient work of becoming someone whose character can be trusted across every domain of life. The sages maintained that posture, and the wisdom they accumulated and preserved is the record of what such a posture, practiced faithfully over time, eventually produces.

For readers who now return to Proverbs with this broader understanding in place, the book is likely to feel different than it did before. Sayings that once seemed self-evident may now reveal layers of meaning that a first reading missed. Passages that once felt demanding may now be recognizable as honest descriptions of what genuine wisdom requires — and as genuine encouragements that it is worth pursuing. The book will continue to give back more as the reader continues to bring more to it.

The invitation Proverbs extends has not changed across the centuries. It is the same invitation it has always been: to pursue wisdom seriously, to receive it humbly, to express it in the daily texture of one's relationships and responsibilities, and to remain genuinely open to continued growth — trusting that what wisdom produces, over time, in a life genuinely committed to its pursuit, is worth more than anything else one might have chosen to invest in instead.

That conversation began long before any of us. It will continue long after. Proverbs endures because the questions it carries are not going away, and because the posture of humble, attentive, persistent wisdom it models is one that every generation has found it necessary to learn again.

The Bible for Modern Life Series

This book is part of **The Bible for Modern Life** series—an ongoing collection that explores the meaning, historical setting, and message of individual books of Scripture.

Each volume looks closely at the biblical text to help readers understand what it meant in its original context and how its truths still apply to life today.

The goal is simple: to help modern readers engage more deeply with the Bible—one book at a time.

— Samuel Whitaker